Praise for *Second Person, Possessive*

William Henderson's *Second Person, Possessive* is a brutally honest memoir that is at times harrowing, poignant and heartbreaking, yet always compelling. I expect we will hear more from this exceptional writer in the future.

Paul Alan Fahey, ed. *The Other Man: 21 Writers Speak Candidly About Sex, Love, Infidelity, & Moving On*

Second Person, Possessive illuminates life's most intense moments of love, heartbreak, and madness. Written with unflinching clarity, Henderson ties a knot you have to keep reading to unravel. His voice urges understanding of himself, life and all those he loves.

Noriko Nakada, author of *Through Eyes Like Mine* and *Overdue Apologies*

William Henderson knows intimately that there are truths in contradiction and that there are always (at least) two sides of a story. *Second Person Possessive* is a gripping story that does what I love best in literature: wrestles with shadow, cuts to the quick, and deepens my understanding of the messy complexity of human relationships. This is a book you will be compelled to read in one sitting, a book you'll think about many days after you've finished. Prepare to descend.

Wendy C. Ortiz, author of *Hollywood Notebook*

Second Person Possessive is a haunting exploration into the idea of weaving: to negotiate the creation of unexpected worlds and desires, the insertion of lives into other lives. Will serves as author and interlacer of this memoir—the characters here must be stitched together and it is up to Will to do it: through delicate thread, through glue, through lies, through addiction, through love that is both abundant and scarce. This is a story of trying to share a life with others while the world, as well as inner anxieties, want to keep things quiet. The result is harrowing and beautiful—an attempt to reinvent a life while simultaneously trying to reinvent what it means to be a lover, a father, a human being.

Brian Oliu, author of *Level End* and *So You Know It's Me*

Second Person Possessive is proof that life can become a carnival of chaos, how we steer ahead with only our hearts and how the universe can throw sucker punches. This debut is expertly crafted and quite perfect in many ways, quite unlike you and I.

Michael Graves, author of *Dirty One*

You'll read this book and you'll find yourself stripping it down layer by layer. First, you will pull apart the individual pieces, and there you will find honesty. Then you will pull apart the sentences, and in them you will find painstaking clarity. And then you will get down to each and every raw, often agonizing word, and there you will find William Henderson, a rich and crushing storyteller. This is the memoir to consume slowly, and again and again.

Andrew Keating, author of *Participants*

Second Person, Possessive

Second Person, Possessive

William Henderson

Ash Press

Published in the United States by Ash Press, Boston

ISBN: 978-0-615-90161-9

Printed in the United States of America

2 4 6 8 9 7 5 3 1

First Edition

Book design by William Henderson

Author photograph copyright © 2013 by Holly Henderson

For Avery, who was there

&

For Aurora, who was on her way

Author's note

Second Person, Possessive is a work of non-fiction. To write this book, I relied on my memory of specific events and also on journals, text messages, e-mails and letters. When I could, I consulted with the people who appear in the book. I have changed the names of most but not all of the individuals in this book, and I have modified identifying characteristics in some cases to preserve anonymity. There are neither composite characters nor composite events in this book, though I omitted people and events when doing so did not affect the veracity or substance of the story.

How a Clock Without Hands Tells Time

I sent him text after text after text, each more desperate than the one before it, each making promises I couldn't really keep, and he, my boyfriend, Jay, kept me at arm's length. At phone's length. Until he didn't. And had he simply texted *The End* I may not have understood any more than I did—than I do—but I would have given him props for the text message.

Don't call me. Don't text me. We're done. We're over. We're through.

My world collapsed, playing cards tossed out of a simple deck. Fifty-two pieces of shiny paper floating to the floor. Light as a feather, stiff as a board. Shards of glass where a window had been. You think I'm exaggerating, but I'm not.

You'll see. Nothing about this is an exaggeration.

I'm talking to you but I'm also talking to a psychiatrist—Kathy, she said in introduction—the fifth psychiatrist I've talked to since I signed myself into St. Elizabeth's for a 72-hour inpatient observation.

I tried twice to kill myself.

That's not an exaggeration either.

"What brings you here, Bill?"

My name is not Bill. She must know why I'm here. She likely read the notes that the other psychiatrists took.

I hate her already.

Talking to the first psychiatrist was difficult, the story still bottled in me, waiting to be heard. The story, then, still filled with secrets and mysteries, a lock waiting to be turned. When I talked to that psychiatrist, I was still living the story.

"Bill," Kathy asks again.

"Will," I say, probably more harshly than I should, "My name is Will."

"Will," Kathy says.

She makes a note of it on one of several pieces of paper she has in her lap.

Wonder what else has been written about me. And what my wife, Holly, is doing and if our son, Avery, knows he'll see me later and what my boyfriend—ex-boyfriend—Jay is doing and what time it is.

Wife. Boyfriend. Ex-boyfriend. Son.

You'll get to know them in time. You may even feel sorry for one or more of them. Just remember that Jay and I will get back together. I'm convinced of it. He told me that he couldn't imagine a life without me in it. Those text messages he sent, well, he didn't really mean them.

I wonder what he's doing right now. He's probably at work, not that I know what time it is or even what day. No, I know what day it is. Or I could know, if I thought about it. We are not allowed watches in here, and there are no clocks. Well, no working clocks. A clock with no hands hangs in the main room, where the nurses' station is and where they calculate our allotment of medication.

Today could be Monday or Tuesday or Thursday next week.

I'm in St. Elizabeth's Medical Center in Brighton, Massachusetts, a hospital once synonymous with mental health care for young adults. Somewhere in the hospital is a rusted iron lung and rooms where children met with therapists and psychiatrists and took pills to make them big and small and big again. Chalkboards with faded fingerprints and window blinds hanging half open on dusty windows. Entire wings of the hospital shuttered and closed, forgotten. Stories of screams and screamers, forgotten. Closed.

And I'm meeting with Kathy. She's probably in her late forties and has a slight accent. She looks at me and crosses her legs. The papers in her lap make the sound paper makes when it rubs against other sheets of paper.

"Can you tell me what brought you to St. Elizabeth's?" Kathy asks.

The glib answer is my wife brought me here.

Other answers are more complicated.

I'm 33, and people have been calling me a faggot since I was 10, when I asked during sex education if two men could make a baby together. The rumors followed me from elementary school through middle school and again through high school and college. I couldn't be gay, I said, since I was attracted to women, and dated them, albeit unsuccessfully. Didn't stop the rumors and the name-calling and how some people wouldn't walk on the same side of the hall with me in case I had AIDS. Learned to ignore the rumors, but couldn't ignore the underlying message that who I am and what I wanted is wrong.

"Are you thinking about killing yourself today?" Kathy asks. She must have given up on my answering her other question.

"Not today," I say.

"Did you think about killing yourself yesterday?" she asks.

"Not yesterday, either," I say.

"But last week you did," Kathy says.

So today is Monday.

Five days ago, everything broke, when I felt like I was falling into a black hole. Going supernova. Exploding.

Multiple explosions since the text message from Jay ending our relationship, the text message that should have just said *The End* instead of all of the hateful things his text messages said.

Five days since the text message and the pills. Attempt number one.

Four days since the bridge. Attempt number two.

Three days since Holly suggested I sign myself into St. Elizabeth's.

Measure time in sleeps and moments and the number of hours between seeing and seeing again. Bats in the belfry and keys to his home and the side of his bed that he called my side of the bed. Made his bed before I left that last morning. Took him lunch during his break. Called him that night. And called and called. He didn't pick up and eventually turned off his phone.

My thoughts shouldn't be this twisted, not when I'm far removed from what twisted them.

"Have you tried to kill yourself before?" Kathy asks.

"No," I say.

"Did you want to die?"

14

Sorry, Kathy. Can't talk to you about the ending without telling you about the beginning. Only then will you understand why the stakes felt so high and why I felt like my only play was to commit suicide.

Someone said once that a love story with two sides is not so much a love story as it is a tragedy. I know someone said that, yet if you Google that phrase, or a variation of it, none of the more than 105 million results that appear in less than .20 seconds is that exact phrase. Maybe I read it, or maybe it's a line of dialogue from a movie that no one has added to IMDB. But you'd expect that line of dialogue is easily IMDB-able. A love story with two sides is not so much a love story as it is a tragedy. Definitely IMDB-able.

I should tell Kathy that I didn't want to die, but I would be lying. And I've done enough of that.

Magical Tales of Impossible Events

1

Jay and I met six-and-a-half months ago. Snow on the ground. Ice. For weeks, Jay and I, having crossed paths online months earlier, had circled each other and this night. We exchanged information like we were upping the ante in a high-stakes game of poker.

Our conversations leapfrogged from art to books to music to sex. We described what we liked and were willing to do under the right circumstances and with the right person. The early e-mails with Jay, sentences and questions and unlocked photos. Promises to share more later.

I didn't tell him about my wife or son. I've never been much of a gambler.

He left out part of his story, too.

Jay lived about three miles away from the home that Holly and I share. On a map, the town where he lives and the town where I live fit together the way that bodies can, inside and on top of, surrounding.

Before going to meet him, I had two rum-and-Cokes. More rum than Coke. No ice. I took two showers and changed my clothes three times before putting on what I had worn to work that day. Put on new underwear, though.

Jay knew what he was getting, as did I. He and I had swapped photos—he is two inches taller than me, shaves his head, has a tattoo of the Buddha on his back, and blue eyes

Three times I got lost driving to Jay's apartment. Only after pulling over to side of the road and reloading the directions into the maps app on my phone did I realize I had passed the street I needed to take.

Some of the homes on the street where he lives were lit with Christmas lights. Snow on sidewalks and in banks made by plows. Checked the number of the building against the number he had given me twice before texting Jay to let him know I was there.

"Where should I park?" I asked.

"Anywhere," Jay responded.

The driveway in front of Jay's apartment was full.

I slid more than parked in what I thought was a space, the back of my car extending over a sidewalk, but I couldn't tell, given how much snow was on the ground.

I stood outside of my car, snow soaking through the legs of my pants and my shoes and my socks. He had asked me to bring wine and chocolate and I brought both. Had to be bold, coming over, bringing gifts, expecting to get laid.

I wasn't used to sleeping with men, or cheating on my wife, or spending weeks flirting with a man I met online. Chatting late at night, after Holly and Avery were asleep. Trying not to laugh or speak out loud while talking to the other men who preceded Jay and then to Jay.

Not telling these men that I am married was unfair, but they likely were as unfair with me. Online, you can be anyone and promise to do anything and make plans that often go unrealized.

Standing outside of my car, my feet wet and cold. The porch light of Jay's home came on, and then he came outside.

"I'm Jay," he said.

I hadn't expected him to have a British accent.

"I'm Will," I said.

"Come on up," he said.

He waited for me to walk inside the building before closing the door and turning off the porch light.

"We're on the third floor," he said.

He was taller than I had expected.

I walked in front of him up the stairs, and I wondered if he was looking at my ass, since he was walking behind me.

I would have looked at his ass, had he been walking in front of me.

His front door, the only door on the third floor, was open. I waited for him to walk in first, which he did, and as we walked down a hallway, he pointed out the different rooms. Living room. Roommate's bedroom. Bathroom. Second roommate's bedroom. The hallway connected to a combined kitchen/dining room, which smelled like someone had been cooking. To get to Jay's bedroom, you have to walk through the kitchen. We walked into his bedroom and he closed his bedroom door.

I took in what I could of his bedroom. His bed was in the middle of the room, while a desk, chair, and computer were opposite it. Shelves filled with books and CDs hung on each wall. A plant, a cross-legged Buddha statue, and an incense holder were positioned next to each other on a table I later learned he calls his altar.

Three candles were lit, one of which smelled like sandalwood. It was a votive.

"Do you want some wine?" he asked, motioning to a carafe on his desk. Two glasses were next to it, one filled halfway. "I may have already had one or two glasses."

"I had drinks before coming over, too" I said.

He poured me a glass of wine, and I put down the bottle I brought.

Jay looked at the bottle.

"Let's finish what I poured first," he said.

I picked my copy based on its label.

I sat in the chair at his desk, and he sat cross-legged in his bed.

I took off my shoes. My socks were wet, and I wanted to take them off, but I knew if I did, my feet would be cold and I'd end up asking him to borrow a pair of socks, and of everything we probably would do, wearing his socks might end up being the most personal.

"Can we put on some music?" I asked.

"You choose," he said.

I picked music I think is sexy. With music playing, this preamble to having sex with a man I just met no longer felt awkward.

We talked for more than four hours, and I was tired and not tired, and I didn't know how to ask him if he still wanted to fool around, and I thought that maybe we wouldn't fool around, that maybe he had changed his mind.

"It's getting late," he said.

"We've been talking all night."

It was nearly three in the morning.

Then, and for days later, I held onto the things he told me, memorizing each fact and story. I don't remember now the things we talked about.

And now I'm in a hospital, telling Kathy about the night my affair with Jay began. And he has probably invited someone over and already poured that man wine and asked him about hooking up.

Nearly three in the morning and we were no closer to having sex than we had been before I came over.

"Did you still want to hook up?" he asked.

Of course I still wanted to hook up, when he asked me if I still wanted to hook up.

I got out of the chair where I'd been sitting and got into bed with him. He was on the right side of the bed, and I was on the left side of the bed. We were on our sides, facing each other.

I reached for his face, and I kissed him.

I kissed his chest, and down his stomach, and then I pulled at his belt, and he was unbuttoning my jeans, and I was sucking in my stomach so he could take off my jeans and underwear.

The lights were off, and candlelight was not enough to bring everything into focus, and I was doing all of this by touch, and my eyes were closed because I wanted to feel that moment.

I pulled away from him.

"I want to see you again," I said. I couldn't go further without him knowing I wanted more than this one night.

"I want to see you again, too," he said.

I kissed him, and I thought how well our mouths and bodies fit together.

Frantic and rushed and I could feel the wine and the rum-and-Cokes from earlier and we were kissing and we were more than kissing and we were touching each other and more than touching each other and naked and hard and sweating and more than sweating.

"I'm going to clean up," he said, after. He walked out of his bedroom and to the bathroom. I expected him to ask me to leave when he came back.

While he was getting dressed, I got dressed. I picked up the shirt he had been wearing, and I put it in my pants pocket. I put on my coat, to hide the bulge his shirt made in my pants. In case I never saw him again, I wanted something of his.

"I thought you might stay the night," he said when he walked into his bedroom.

"I can't," I said.

He put on a sweater that he took out of his closet. He put on his pants.

He walked me to the front door of the apartment.

"We'll talk soon," he said, and the way he said *we'll talk soon* sounded more like a question than a statement.

"I'm counting on it," I said.

He kissed me goodbye, and his kiss, the way we kissed, felt comfortable.

I pulled away.

"Goodbye, White Rabbit," I said.

I had forgotten his name and called him White Rabbit since he had told me earlier, while we talked about the upcoming film version of *Alice in Wonderland*, that of all of the characters in it, he is most like the rabbit, always leading people places. Spend enough time with him, he said, and I'd learn it was true.

"Goodbye," he said.

2

You're judging me. You're not supposed to, sitting there, taking notes, finding out what brought me here. But you're judging me all the same. Cheating on my wife, and with a man whose name I couldn't remember. Let me keep going. Cheating on my wife, who I have been in a relationship with for 12 years, is only one of my crimes.

3

Even before Avery was born, after Holly and I learned that we needed to use in-vitro fertilization to conceive a child, she and I were no longer connecting.

She worked nights, and I worked days, and we'd text each other reminders about dentist appointments and when we were out of milk and ice cream. She'd pack my lunch when she got home, and I'd make dinner for her before I went to bed. Then we rearranged our lives to accommodate our son. Holly started working weekends so she could have two days off during the week, sacrificing what little time we had been able to spend together.

None of this was how she and I had imagined our lives being when she and I were in college, dating, and then engaged, everything an open road in front of us. No wrong turns, when you're 21 and in love and convinced that you and she can conquer the world. That no one understands you the way she does. That nothing will change, even as you're trying like hell to make everything around you change. To stop needing to use credit cards. To live in an apartment bigger than the one before it. And then you're paying a mortgage and have fully paid for two cars, and you have a child, maybe two.

In vitro. A loft with no walls. Never having a day off from work together. Realizing that I couldn't try any longer to make a physical relationship with a woman work. These things, and a million other pieces of a life we hastily decided to tie together, forgotten in the wake of meeting Jay.

Even before Jay and I met, we were on a collision course for each other.

Fated, Jay says. Or said. Used to say. Won't say again.

Kathy. Sitting there. Watching.

"So you decided to have an affair," she says, more statement than question.

"It wasn't an affair," I say. "He and I were together."

"You were married, and you sought out someone else with whom you had sex. You were having an affair," Kathy says.

"I wouldn't call it an affair."

Nothing about my time with him felt like an affair. I wasn't cheating on Holly, since she and I were no longer having sex—and not having sex with her meant that I wasn't cheating on Jay either.

"What would you call it then?" she asks. Kathy takes off her glasses. I can see a red dent on her nose where her glasses sit. She should get those adjusted.

If not an affair, if not something that sounds like it was meant to end, then why am I here with her?

"I fell in love with him," I said.

Five days after the night I met him, while he and I were each at work, I asked him if he wanted to go out on a real date. Where he worked and where I worked and where he lived and where I lived, all within three miles of each other. I texted him, and then I put my phone facedown on my desk to keep from staring at it and waiting for his response.

But he responded almost immediately.

"Do you still want to go out with me?"

"Yes."

"Dinner on Friday?"

"OK," I said.

During that second date, while waiting for takeaway sushi to be prepared, he confessed that he is a crystal meth addict. Doesn't use anymore, he said. Not meth anyway. Pot, but only when he had it.

Later, he told me that he could tell his confession freaked me out. So he amended it, promising that he would never again use crystal meth, that he had kicked the habit.

"But promise that you will stop me from using, if you think I'm about to," he said. "Promise me that you'll do whatever stopping me takes."

"I promise," I told him.

It was cold and I wasn't dressed appropriately, not knowing that our plans included walking from his apartment to a nearby sushi restaurant and then waiting outside for our order. He knew I was cold. He took his scarf off and wrapped it around my neck, and then he kissed me.

I believed him when he said he was no longer an addict and that he seldom used drugs.

I also thought that his asking me to promise to help him meant that he expected me to be around.

I liked that the most about that conversation—that and the very public kiss. The takeaway sushi was good, too.

We made a third date, and on that third date, we didn't decide to have a fourth as much as we just knew that a fourth date was inevitable.

That we were becoming inevitable.

Holly never questioned why I was out late, when I was out with Jay. Holly just thought I was working.

The day after my third date with Jay, which was ten days after we met, Jay asked me via a text message if I wanted to be in a monogamous relationship with him.

He called it *dating it out*.

I read that text message and I read it again. I was at home, sitting on a couch, watching television, while nearby, Holly and Avery put a puzzle together. I thought about how alike my son and wife look. Holly, five-four, red hair, hazel eyes, freckles. Lots of freckles. Thin. Beautiful, most would say. I say she's beautiful. She is. And our son, Avery, his hair turning more auburn the older he gets. The first of what will likely be many freckles already showing. Hazel eyes.

Yes, I texed back to Jay.

He asked me to date it out, and I said yes—and that's how everything began, if you need me to pinpoint a beginning.

We must have talked more that night. Made plans. We must have, because that's the sort of thing we did.

He likely called me his boyfriend.

He liked labeling things.

I think his need to label was really his way of creating order in his life. You are this and you are this and you are this and now you are not this.

Order where before there was only chaos.

And then we started seeing each other as often as we could. Knowing Holly would never believe I was working, those nights I planned to be with Jay, I told her a little about having a new friend, a man I met at work. I think she enjoyed being home alone with Avery, so again, she never questioned why I was around even less than I had been.

And Jay, well, I don't think he expected an invitation to my home straight away, so I didn't feel bad, being unable to invite him. And I didn't feel bad when, after spending an evening together, I told him that I couldn't stay the night. He didn't make me feel bad about that either, at least not at first.

He and I didn't reveal everything about ourselves to each other at once. We volleyed questions like *when was your heart last broken* and *have you ever cried until you felt something inside you break* and *when was the last time you knew you hurt someone*. We traded answers a bit more slowly. Benefit of texting questions like these is that you can take longer to respond than you can in person.

He described living in Texas and North Carolina. There was a stint at a boarding school in London. I never asked him why his parents sent him away, and I don't know how long he boarded at that school. Long enough to pick up an accent, and that was about as much as I thought about his stories of going to school in London.

While living in Texas, things got to be more than he could handle, so he moved back in with his mother, who lived in Peoria. He wasn't close to his brother, didn't talk to his father, and called a woman that his mother helped raise, his sister, even though his mother never adopted this woman.

"You'll meet her one day," Jay said with such certainty that I believed that I would meet her, even though she lives in Illinois.

To shift his attention from asking me questions that I couldn't answer without lying, I often asked him to tell me stories that he hadn't told anyone. And, failing that, to make up stories that he hadn't yet made up.

Jay has scars on his arms, higher up than his wrists. Horizontal scars. One scar is darker and larger than the other scar. I had noticed the scars the first night we spent time together, and had spent time kissing and sucking on those scars.

One night, I asked him about them.

"I don't know how to tell you everything," he said. "I'm going to sound awful."

"Are the scars one of your awful stories?"

"I kind of wanted to know what bleeding out felt like, and I kind of wanted to stop feeling. So I cut one arm, but I didn't cut deep enough. And then I cut my other arm, and I cut too deep. But I'm not suicidal or anything like that."

"I'm not suicidal or anything either," I said.

I likely kissed his scars after he told me that story. We probably fooled around.

5

We started spending Friday nights together. I would meet him at his apartment after we both finished work. He would make dinner, or we would order out. I'd often bring over a movie for us to watch. Sometimes we made it all the way through the movies; other times, we got distracted.

One Friday night, he had made dinner and begged me to stay. I told him I couldn't. He got high in front of me that night. He asked me if I wanted to smoke, but I don't like pot and told him that I was fine if he did it by himself. I must have fallen asleep watching him smoke because the next thing I knew, I was waking up and it was light outside and I knew I was in trouble. Holly would never believe that I had stayed out with friends until—I looked at my phone and saw it was after 5 in the morning.

"Where are you going?" Jay asked.

"I have to go home," I told him. "Why'd you let me fall asleep?"

"I tried to wake you up," he said. He reached for his phone, which he used as his alarm clock. "I set an alarm for 6, because I know you have things to do."

What he didn't know is I had to be home to be with Avery so Holly could go to work.

After getting home and telling Holly that I had gotten drunk at a friend's house and thought sleeping for a few hours was better than driving, I called Jay. I asked him when I had fallen asleep.

"I think you got a little high," he said. "Secondhand and all."

I haven't thought about that night in a while, but I think that was the night he admitted that he more than liked to smoke pot and would do it every day if he could.

Which he couldn't, he claimed, since he only smoked pot when he had it.

What I only learned later is that he always has it. That he lets his roommate pay for his share of some bills with pot. That his roommate is a dealer. That he and his roommate slept together. That his roommate's boyfriend doesn't know that they used to sleep together.

All of these things I didn't know, not until later, and yet what he didn't know—what I didn't tell him—seems so much worse.

The more of this story I tell Kathy, the more certain I am that she will absolve me and tell me I had no choice but to do what I did, which, ultimately, ended the very thing I wanted not to end.

"When did you tell him about your son?" Kathy asks.

That's a good question. I hadn't planned to introduce him to Avery, but I was also running out of reasons to explain why I couldn't stay the night with him.

And I liked him.

I more than liked him.

And I thought he more than liked me.

I decided one Sunday afternoon, when Holly wasn't home, that if Jay and I had a chance—I still think we have a chance, despite everything—but if he and I had a chance, then I had to introduce him to Avery and wait and see how he reacted to dating someone who has a child.

I brought Avery with me to Jay's apartment. I texted him, when we got there. By the time I got to the front door of Jay's apartment, he was standing there, and I saw him see me holding a child.

He stepped away from the door and followed me up the stairs. I didn't wonder if he was watching my ass; I wondered if he was wondering how soon he could ask me to leave. I walked inside Jay's apartment, and then down the hallway, and then into the kitchen where Jay's roommates—his dealer, Tyrese, and Annie, a woman who worked with Jay—were eating.

Avery pulled himself out of my arms, and introduced himself to each of the roommates. Or what passed for an introduction from a two-year-old. Mostly he hugged their legs and asked to be picked up.

"Who's the baby?" Annie asked.

"He's my son," I said.

"No shit," Tyrese said.

"Yeah," I said. "He's two. His name is Avery."

Jay stood at the doorway to his bedroom, not saying anything. Avery ran into Jay's bedroom and I followed. Jay closed the door behind us. Avery bee-lined for Jay's bookshelves, took off several books from the shelves, lost interest, and climbed into the chair in front of Jay's desk. While there, he started tapping the keys on Jay's computer keyboard.

Jay watched.

"Up," Avery said. He was looking at Jay, who was looking at Avery. I was looking at both of them.

"Up," Avery repeated.

Jay picked up Avery, who hugged Jay's neck.

"I don't know how to entertain a small child," Jay said.

Jay wrapped his arms around Avery, who was still hugging Jay's neck.

Jay chose a cartoon in his movie library, and sat in the chair near his computer. Avery sat in Jay's lap, and when the movie came on, Avery stopped moving and focused on the movie.

"How?" Jay asked.

I stayed as close to the truth as I could.

"I'm raising Avery with a woman named Holly. She's my best friend. She and I met in college. We live together and co-parent Avery. We've talked about a second child.

30

We've also talked about raising children while living in separate homes."

She and I hadn't yet talked about living apart.

We have now.

I never considered telling Jay the whole truth.

"I'll have to meet her," Jay said.

"Yeah," I said, sounding as non-committal as I thought I could sound without arousing suspicion.

"I knew there was something you were hiding. Is there anything else?"

I watched how Jay held Avery, and how Jay wrapped his arms tight around Avery, and how Avery made himself comfortable in Jay's lap. I thought that if things with him went the way they had been going, then Jay and I would end up spending our lives together raising Avery with Holly.

"No," I said. "I'm not hiding anything else."

When the movie ended, I said I had to take Avery home.

"I'll see you later?" I asked.

"Yes," Jay said.

About five minutes after I left, Jay texted: *I still take you and your son, as is. I'm not scared. I'm not going anywhere.*

6

When you think about having an affair, or while you're in the middle of having an affair, you tend to not think about the very things you should think about.

Like how many times you may have to eat dinner twice, because you want to have dinner with both people. Or where you'll hide your wedding ring, when you're with the person with whom you're having the affair.

I put my wedding ring in the ashtray of my car, when Jay and I were together.

You don't think about how the one lie—I'm single and would like to date you—is a multi-headed hydra of lies that isn't easily unlied once lied.

You stop sleeping, because you try to give time to both of the people in your life.

You can't introduce the other person to your friends, no matter how often he or she asks.

And you are never prepared for the guilt, even if you think you are not prone to feeling guilty.

Jay switched his schedule at work so he, Avery, and I could spend Saturday and Sunday morning and afternoon together while Holly was at work. His rearranged schedule made spending a weekend evening together impossible.

"He's as much part of this as you or I am," Jay would say. "And I like him. A lot. Almost as much as I like you."

At least at first Jay would say these things. Then the like became love, and the love became more than love.

I acted as if everything wasn't built inside a shifting house of cards. One-eyed jacks, the ones with knives through their heads, and the all-knowing jokers with bags of tricks belted at their waists. The twos and threes and sevens. Those even- and odd-numbered cards are worth nothing, until they are worth everything.

Kathy, in her chair, and me, still in the office.

"You trusted Jay with your son?" Kathy asks.

"I trusted him. He loved Avery. I never doubted the things he said about one day wanting to be Avery's other father."

"He used drugs," Kathy says.

And there is that same fact that has been repeated to me in a number of ways since checking myself into St. Elizabeth's. Jay used drugs, and I didn't use drugs, and regardless of my marriage, I have a child and why would I want to bring my child around someone who uses drugs? Why would I expect to have much of a future with someone who uses drugs? Holly asked those same questions, when I confessed to her the extent of my relationship with Jay; she wanted to know why I spent so much time with someone who used.

"He never used around Avery," I tell Kathy.

"Never?"

"Well, once, but he used before Avery and I went over to his home, and once we got there and I realized that Jay was stoned, I took Avery away."

Father of the year, that's me.

That day, when Avery and I got to Jay's apartment, he was in the shower. I could smell the pot, so I left the breakfast I had made Jay, and I took Avery home.

After Jay saw the breakfast I left him, he texted.

"Were you just here?"

"Yeah."

"Why didn't you stay?"

"You're high, and I have Avery with me."

"I'm not that high."

"I can't have him there when you're high," I texted.

"I just didn't want to feel," he said. "My head just hurts all the time."

We didn't know then how important his head hurting would be; we just knew that he was starting to get headaches aspirin didn't help.

"Was it harder, once Jay started bonding with Avery?" Kathy asks.

"No," I say. "I loved Jay, and he loved me."

"Don't you think you loved him kind of quickly?" she asks. "It was only a few months, right?"

"Six-and-a-half months," I say, like that extra two weeks means anything at this point.

It will, I think. We're just taking a break, and in a few days, or maybe a bit longer, he and I will get back together, and we won't start over from zero as much as we'll just not count this time apart.

"And isn't that kind of fast to know you want to spend your life with someone?"

"It didn't feel fast," I say.

"So how did it feel?" Kathy asks.

"It felt—" I want to end the sentence with the word *right*, since he and I felt right from the beginning, but Kathy interrupts.

"It felt exciting, and he made you feel special, and Holly hadn't made you feel special in a while."

"That's true," I say. I know I'm ceding much ground with that admission.

Green Alien

1

Our one-month anniversary fell on Valentine's Day, a difficult-enough holiday for a recently coupled couple even without the pressure of celebrating an anniversary. Jay and I made plans to have dinner together and he also asked if we could do something with Avery, too.

"I got him a couple of things," Jay said, when he asked if he and I could celebrate twice—once alone and once with Avery.

I almost told him I loved him, when he told me he wanted to include Avery in our Valentine's Day plans.

In my head, I often told him I loved him. Those imagined conversations sometimes ended with us in bed and sometimes ended with me telling him that I loved him but couldn't be with him and sometimes ended with him telling me he didn't love me.

But I knew that was unlikely to be his response. The things he told me convinced me that if he didn't already love me, then he soon would.

"I used to think I would need to find two people," he said one night. "I didn't think I would find one man who could challenge me mentally and emotionally and physically. I had given up, or just about given up. I was tired of trying. I was tired of trying and failing."

"You've let me in," I said.

"I can't help but let you in. I shouldn't tell you that, but I can't help it. I hope I'm not making a mistake."

When he said *I hope I'm not making a mistake*, his voice cracked.

"Do you believe in the one?" I asked. I unbuttoned a button on his shirt, which let me more easily put my hand under his shirt and then under his tank top.

"The one?"

"The one person we're meant to find and love?"

"Yes, I believe in the one."

"I think I'm still looking for mine," I said.

Which may have been one of the more honest things I said to Jay.

"Me too," he said, "but I think I'm getting close to finding him."

That night after dinner, when I was getting ready to leave, he asked me to wait until after he went to the bathroom. Now that he knew about Avery, my leaving on Friday nights, even at 2 or 3 in the morning, no longer bothered him. He knew I had to be home so Holly could go to work. He also knew that some eight or nine hours after I left, I'd be back with Avery. That was our Friday and Saturday routine.

He went to the bathroom, and I put on my shoes. I love him, I thought. I love him. And I thought about telling him when he walked me to the door, but I was afraid that if I told him, then he would say it too, and how could I really leave after the first time we said I love you?

While he was in the bathroom, I wrote *I love you* on a piece of paper, and when I went to the bathroom after him, I hid the paper under a towel in his linen closet.

I didn't tell him about the note until I was already halfway home. Stopped at a red light, I texted to him: *Look in your bathroom*, and he responded: *Look in your bag*.

While I had been in the bathroom, or maybe at some point earlier in the evening, he had written *I love you* on a piece of paper and left it for me in my bag.

At home, in the bed she once shared with me, Holly slept, and next to her, tucked into her body, Avery, his head on Holly's breasts, slept too. Standing in the kitchen, reading and re-reading Jay's note, I ate several pieces of the pizza Holly made for dinner, and I watched my family sleep.

2

I don't know how much you want to know. How often we did it, or where? How I'd leave work at lunch, pick him up, take him home, and we'd have sex before going back to work. Long lunches, we called these afternoon trysts. How we never settled into just one way of doing it. How each time felt a little exciting and a little familiar, but never boring.

But if what Jay and I had was an affair, and I guess I'm vacillating between believing that and not believing that, then maybe our affair's point of no return happened the night he and I had sex-sex for the first time.

Jay and I used condoms that first time, in his bed, a Friday night, one week after the *I love you* notes. He told me he had bought the condoms that afternoon, though maybe he lied. Maybe the condoms we used were condoms he bought to use with someone else. I didn't ask, because none of that mattered. I was the one he was putting the condom on, and I was the one he was pulling inside of him. I was the one who fit inside of him. And after, when he asked me if it was OK, I told him that I loved him.

It was the first time either of us had said the words out loud.

"I've been waiting for you to say it," he said.

"You could have said it first."

"I needed you to say it first," he said.

Kathy interrupts.

"How long had you known him at this point?"

"I'd known him five weeks or so," I say.

"Five weeks or so," she repeats.

"I knew I loved Holly in about the same amount of time," I say.

"Had you and he talked about how his drug use bothered you?" Kathy asked.

And because Kathy likely knows everything I've told the other doctors since I've been here, she knows how much Jay's drug use bothered me, and how little he cared that it did.

"We talked about it," I told her. "We made a deal. He would quit as soon as we were living together, because he didn't want to smoke around Avery."

"That was enough for you?"

"I was lying to him. I hadn't told him I was married. And he never made me use with him."

"And that was enough for you?" Kathy repeats.

"I thought if I pushed him on his drug use and asked him to smoke less or even stop that he would tell me no or, even worse than that, break up with me."

"Would that have been such a bad thing?"

"I didn't want to lose him," I said. "I already expected that I would, since I wouldn't use with him."

38

"Never?" Kathy asks.

I amend my answer.

"I got high with him one time."

I kind of liked it, when I agreed to smoke with him, and I liked it even more when he and I had sex. It was different and he was different and I felt like I could be different. That I was the person he thought I was. I liked being stoned and then when he and I were finished, I didn't like being stoned, and I told him I wouldn't smoke with him again.

"Do you think you have a drug problem?" Kathy asks.

"If I liked getting high with him, then he and I wouldn't have ended up where we ended up. And I wouldn't have done what I did."

"Don't you think you're here for reasons other than he used drugs and you didn't?"

"No. That was the flaw in the relationship."

"*That* was the flaw?" Kathy asks.

I know I'm telling her the story of me with—and without—Jay out of order, but I'm telling the story the only way I know how to tell the story. What happened before and what happened during and what happened after and what is happening now.

"You know he never was going to stop using," Kathy says.

She's right. I knew he was never going to stop using, and I continued dating him anyway.

The lies. All of the lies. Both of us, lying when we said *I love you* and lying when we didn't say *I love you* and lying when we said we'd live together one day and raise children together and ever-after happily.

As if Jay and I were playing tennis with our lies.

In tennis, love means you scored nothing. I read somewhere that using love for zero in tennis came from the idea that doing something for love is doing something for nothing. The other scores, fifteen, thirty, forty, sixty based on a clock's face.

"Will," Kathy repeats. "He never would have stopped."

"He would have. He told me he would."

"He would have just started using somewhere else, and then he would have gotten mad at you for making him use somewhere else."

"Maybe," I said.

"How are you feeling?" Kathy asks.

"Better than I was," I say. "I wasn't sleeping. I wasn't eating."

"Were you using drugs?"

Why is she asking me again?

"Just that one time."

"Do you drink alcohol?"

"With him I did. A lot. I thought if I could get him drunk, then maybe he wouldn't have a need to get high."

"You haven't had alcohol since you've been here," Kathy says. "Any cravings?"

"Not at all," I say.

"How is your mood?"

"I have my moments," I say.

"How so?"

"I'm sad. And I'm worried about everything that I have to do. And I'm not sure how I'm going to do it all on my own. Jay was supposed to be here for this part."

"You're better off," Kathy says.

"Why?" I ask.

"You were drinking regularly. You were stressed. You weren't eating. You weren't sleeping. Most people wouldn't have held up as long you did. Most people wouldn't have been able to keep it up."

"But I don't know how to turn off what I feel."

I don't want to turn off what I feel.

"You will in time," she says. Then she shifts gears. "Let's talk about medication."

I'm surprised by how willing I am to not only talk about medication but actually take it. I know something is wrong with me. Or in me. In my head. I do things I shouldn't do and I feel things I shouldn't feel and I want things I shouldn't want.

Him. I want him.

I want him back, and I know that I'll get him back. I just need to get out of here, maybe give him some time to cool down. He said I was the one. That we were meant to be together. He'll take me back, and things will be better.

"Will medication help me stay balanced?"

"Do you feel out of balance?"

"Sometimes," I say.

"Do you feel manic? Like everything is happening really fast and everything is out of your control and then you get all this energy and you don't know what to do with it? Or do you get depressed, so you crash, and you don't want to do anything."

"Sometimes, but I'm more manic than depressed."

"And how long do you think you've felt like this?"

"Most of my life," I say.

"I think it's likely that there is an underlying undiagnosed bipolar disorder at play as well."

"Which means what?"

"You have severe mood swings. Periods of manic episodes are followed by depressive episodes, and vice versa. You go from having so much energy you don't know what to do with it all, to not having energy."

"And you think that may have influenced my behavior?"

Maybe if I give Jay a medical reason for why I did what I did, he'll more easily understand. Then I'll tell him I'm treating the condition, and he has nothing to worry about.

"I think you likely experienced situational-based mania. And because you didn't know how to handle everything happening around you, this mania may have influenced some of the decisions you made. But it is not solely responsible for any of the decisions you made. Does that make sense?"

"I'd have made the decisions regardless of feeling manic?"

"Maybe different decisions, and maybe even better decisions, but the mania contributed to how you felt and how you handled the situation."

"And medication will cure me?"

"I wouldn't call it a cure," she says. "Medication will basically level out your brain chemistry. It's kind of like you won't be able to feel anything to the same extreme level that you're used to. The medication will give your brain the something that isn't quite right in your baseline chemistry."

None of what she said makes sense, mostly because everything she said makes sense. As far back as I can remember I've gotten irrationally mad at things that didn't warrant such a response. Holly and I were washing dishes once, something like six or seven years ago, and she dropped a plate while she was drying it. The plate, part of a set, broke. Instead of sweeping the pieces into a dustpan, I dropped two of the three other plates in the set to the ground. They broke too.

"What the fuck?" Holly asked. I think she was frightened.

"You broke part of a set," I said. "No sense having part of something if we can't have the whole thing."

Kathy is still talking.

"Would you want to try lithium? I've had success treating periods of manic episodes with lithium."

"Doesn't it make you gain weight?"

"Sometimes," she says.

"I don't want to trade mood stability for twenty pounds."

"Is weight an issue for you?"

It always has been and likely always will be.

I was an overweight child, and then I was an obese teenager. When the kids I went to school weren't calling me a faggot, they were calling me a fat-fuck.

And then one day I started counting calories and fat grams, measuring portions and drinking only water. Only after I lost 30 pounds did people start noticing. My clothes were baggy and then my pants no longer fit, even with a belt. I went from XL to medium and then even smaller. In 10 months, I lost 110 pounds.

People thought I had AIDS. It was 1993. Back then, people were afraid you could catch AIDS by swimming in a pool that someone with AIDS swam in. Teased for being fat and then teased for not being fat and over the next six or seven years, my weight slowly crept back up.

When I was 25, Holly agreed to help me pay for liposuction. She wanted me to be happy, and she thought

I might like myself more. Five years later, we paid for me to have a tummy tuck, which is less tucking and more cutting. My body is scarred where it was divided then put back together.

After Jay told me the story about the scars on his forearms, when I didn't volunteer the story of my scar, he asked about it one night while we were in the shower.

I told him the story, how my surgeon had cut away the part of my belly with my belly button on it, so he had carved a new button for me.

Jay stuck his finger inside my belly button.

It took everything I had not to pull away from him, touching me the way he was.

"It feels weird," Jay said.

"I could have asked him to leave it off."

"That would have been weirder," Jay said.

We were out of the shower, drying off, when Jay told me that I'm the one who should be proud.

"Why?" I asked.

"You've sculpted a fairly perfect you," he said.

I tell Kathy none of this. Instead, I simply tell her that I've had problems with my weight in the past, weigh more than I would like to, and plan to start a diet as soon as I get other things in my life in order.

"We could try Lamictal, then," Kathy says. "It's not as commonly used to treat bipolar disorder."

"What do people use it for?"

"It was developed to treat seizures in children and adults," she says. "But it was found to also be effective delaying periods of mania common for people with bipolar disorder."

Thinking I have bipolar disorder is unsettling, despite it explaining my mood swings over the years. It sounds like I'm more broken than I feel. She said she thinks the precipitating condition was situational-based mania. That sounds a lot less severe, I think.

"Any side effects?" I ask.

"Sometimes," she says.

"What sort of side effects?"

"Some people develop a severe skin rash, and in a small number of people, pieces of their skin start to fall off. But if I prescribe you Lamictal, and you notice something happening, we would stop immediately."

"Any weight gain?"

"None. It might even help you lose weight. It sometimes curbs appetite."

"I'm up to trying it," I say.

She writes me a prescription.

"Have this filled today, and start taking it tomorrow," she says. "I think you're going to be fine."

I think she has to tell me that she thinks I'm going to be fine, even if fine is far from how she thinks I'm going to be.

Our interview over, she gives me her card.

A Borealis Named Aurora

1

Kathy is psychiatrist number five, but before her was Erin, a woman who isn't a psychiatrist but is somehow responsible for evaluating me during my inpatient hospitalization.

I had been a patient at St. Elizabeth's for about 12 hours when Erin and her intern—a women whose name I can't remember—came to my room and asked to meet with me. We sat at a round table in a communal dining room and talked about the sequence of events that led to my suicide attempts.

We talked about my feelings.

I opted not to tell them that I felt—and still feel—gray.

Do you know what gray feels like?

It feels like locking yourself away in a psychiatric hospital, unsure if you can stand being alive for another day.

It feels like everything in your world has exploded.

It feels like coming out to your wife while confessing an affair with a man whom you wanted to marry.

It feels like you can't remember anyone's name.

Erin, during that initial conversation, explained that part of my rehab included participating in a two-week partial-hospital program, which meets every other day for eight hours a day. To leave the hospital at the end of my 72-hour inpatient stay, then participation was mandatory.

This morning, Monday, a few hours before I should be cleared to check myself out, Erin retrieved me from my room.

I had already packed the bag I brought with me.

"I'll bring you back at lunch, so you can sign the discharge papers," she said. "The program today ends at four, and you can leave after that."

Kathy collected me from the room where the partial-hospital program meets first thing this morning. She returns me to Erin in time for the group to break for lunch. Erin walks me back to the floor where I've been staying. She says she'll come back for me when lunch is over.

I sign myself out and skip lunch.

I wasn't kidding about that diet.

A nurse returns a belt to me that an orderly had confiscated when I checked myself in. Couldn't have it, in case I wanted to hang myself.

My room had been similarly suicide-proofed: No glass in the mirror in the bathroom, and just enough water in the toilet so that it wasn't empty. I guess the hospital wanted to avoid drowning-related deaths.

I sit on a couch and wait for Erin to come back for me. The locked doors and all. The clock with no hands is on the same wall as the couch. Why keep a clock around that no longer tells time?

I can't figure out if this clock with no hands has a deeper meaning, or if someone, at some point, lacking any other way of committing suicide, broke the clock, and then its hands, and used them—or tried to—in an attempt to once and for all stop time.

47

Walking back with Erin to the room where the partial-hospital program meets, I know I will not come back to St. Elizabeth's, to the floor with its orderlies and nurses and social workers who, in ways big and small, helped keep me alive.

"Thank you for helping me feel normal," I tell Erin at the end of the day, because I don't know what else to say. And because I feel more normal now than I have in a while.

Talking to Kathy likely helped as well.

"You're all normal here," Erin says. "You just need some help getting through difficult situations. Everybody needs help sometimes, and you're lucky enough to be in a place where you can get that help."

2

Outside the hospital, a valet asks if I need to pick up a car, and a woman lights up a cigarette far enough away from the entrance to pretend she doesn't see the no-smoking sign. I blink several times because the sun is bright.

Holly picks me up. Avery is in the backseat. He is drinking out of his sippy cup, and wearing swim trunks. Holly tells me they went to the beach.

I ask for my phone.

"He didn't call or text," she says.

"I'm not looking to see if he tried to get in touch with me," I say.

I am looking to see if Jay tried to get in touch with me.

I have two-hundred and four e-mails, mostly junk.

"Were they able to tell you if we're having a boy or a girl?"

"They could tell, and they wrote it down on the back of a sonogram picture," she says. "They put the picture in an envelope."

"Thank you for waiting for me," I say.

"You should be there when we find out."

Holly, around fourteen weeks pregnant with our second child.

Didn't see that coming, did you?

Neither did Jay, when I told him.

3

To conceive Avery, all Holly and I needed to do was one round of in-vitro fertilization. Avery came a bit more than three weeks early, slept once in his crib, and slept between Holly and me until I stopped sleeping in the same bed as Holly.

Several people at St. Elizabeth's asked me how I could try to kill myself knowing that doing so would turn Avery, and the child Holly carried, into half orphans? I told them the same thing I told myself—without me, Holly could move away from Boston, settle near her parents in California, and eventually be happy.

But I know that killing myself would have been the easy way out of the situation, eliminating the need to tell anyone about what I had done or face a life without Jay.

Before I met Jay, Holly and I tried twice to conceive a second child. Neither try took, though the second implantation resulted in a successful pregnancy, at least for a couple of weeks. I was at work when she texted that she was starting to bleed. She told me not to come home. Her parents were visiting. They would take her to her doctor.

She told me later that the pregnancy had ended.

She wouldn't talk about it, not that night, and very little since, other than to say that I couldn't understand what sitting on a toilet and feeling what losing a pregnancy feels like. She told me she collected some of the discharge in a piece of tissue and buried it somewhere in the yard of our condo building. Something else she went through on her own.

The night Holly and I decided to try to have another baby, Jay and I had been dating for about two months. He knew about Avery, and about Holly and these failed attempts, by this point. He asked nearly every day when he could meet her. He told me he loved Avery and couldn't imagine a life without him—or me—in it.

Couldn't imagine it but had no problem making it happen.

That day, Holly had asked if we could have a family date at a Chinese restaurant. She said she was tired of being home with Avery alone all the time. She was tired of cooking. She needed help parenting. Maybe Avery would behave better somewhere other than our home.

I didn't think Avery was the problem. I was—and am—convinced that Holly is responsible for how Avery behaves when the two of them are together. If she more consistently followed through with threatened punishments, maybe Avery's behavior would change.

But I agreed, cancelling plans with Jay to hang out and order take-out.

Sometimes I thought that he knew I was married, and Holly knew I was having an affair, but neither of them was inclined to say so. They let me think I was fooling them, when really the only person I was fooling was myself, thinking that I'd be able to get everything I wanted.

Holly and I sat across from each other in a booth, and Avery was in a highchair. He didn't want to be in his highchair, and he pleaded with Holly to let him out. I suggested we leave Avery where he was. But Holly took Avery out, and once out, Avery refused to settle down. He sat next to Holly, then crawled under the table and over to my side, sitting next to me long enough to swipe a sugar packet, and then he was out and running around the restaurant.

I let Holly get him.

She put Avery back in his highchair, and Avery cried, only stopping once I let him drink some of my iced tea. I held the cup for him, even though he wanted to hold it for himself.

"No, Avery," I said. "Let Daddy hold it."

"Otay, Daddy," he said. And he drank the tea and laughed. I think he laughed because he knew he was not supposed to be drinking iced tea and had yet again defeated us.

"Do you think we should try again?" Holly asked.

I knew what she wanted us to again try. I think I'd been waiting for her to bring it up.

"I'm not sure. We can barely handle one child."

"Avery needs a sibling," she said. "I think he'll calm down and become easier to parent if he has a friend."

Our food came, and we started eating.

"Why are you hesitating?" she asked. "What's making you question this?"

"I'm worried that we'll have another child, and then we'll move into separate houses, and co-parenting two children from two homes seems impossible."

Which is what I said, though what I thought was that Holly would fight me for custody once she learned I am gay, and trying to retain rights to Avery would likely be easier if I wasn't also trying to retain rights to a baby, let alone one that hadn't yet been born.

Holly stopped eating. She said she was done.

I asked our waitress to box up our food. I think she was grateful that we were going to take our food to go. Avery's behavior had disrupted several other groups of people eating nearby. One party even took their food and drinks to another table.

"How do you know if something is worth saving?" Holly asked while I was driving us home.

Avery was falling asleep in the backseat.

"I don't think we are," I said.

"You don't think there's any hope?"

"I don't know."

"How do you know when enough is enough?"

"I don't know," I said.

This is not the conversation that I remember us having, though this is the conversation Holly remembers us having. She brought it up during the second set of visiting hours at St. Elizabeth's. She asked me why I hadn't told her then what I was doing, and I explained my concerns about losing Avery.

"I wouldn't do that," she said.

And I had to agree, given how she was still here with Avery and our unborn child, despite everything.

Holly and I remember the rest of the conversation the same way.

"Would you still want another child, even if you knew we weren't going to live together or raise the children under the same roof?" I asked.

"Yes." She didn't hesitate.

"Then we can try again," I said.

4

I wasn't with Holly, the afternoon our most recent embryo was implanted into Holly. I was in New York with Jay. Since the procedure is outpatient, and something Holly had experienced three times, she told me to go and have a good time. She told me she'd call and let me know how it went.

I drove, since Jay didn't have a car, and we were in Connecticut when Holly texted me a photograph of a grainy ultrasound picture of our embryo. I responded that it had her eyes, and then I put my phone away, caught up in being on an extended road trip with Jay, his hand on my leg, and a CD he made playing in the car.

"What do you think about a second child?" I asked Jay. We had crossed into New York. He had me pull over near a sign that welcomed us to the Empire State.

"What do you mean?" Jay asked.

"Holly and I have been talking about having another baby, and I'm wondering what you think about that."

"I'm not sure," he said. "Two children are a lot."

"They would be."

"And I may want a child of my own someday. Could we raise three of them?"

"I don't know."

I didn't even know if I could raise two children; how could I promise Jay I'd be up to raising three?

And yet I expected him to raise two.

When we got back that night, he asked me if I could come upstairs with him. I thought he wanted to have sex before I left, or that maybe he'd ask me to stay over, but instead he handed me a ring box. Inside were keys to his apartment.

"You're giving me keys to your place?" I asked.

Kathy had interrupted me at this point in my story. She asked if I thought moving in with someone after two months, let alone someone who uses drugs, would have been the smartest idea. I told her I didn't do it, but she countered and said she knew I likely wanted to. She thinks that him asking me to move in so quickly illustrates how unhealthy our relationship is—was. No one knows after a few weeks that they want to spend their lives with someone. She said that he and I clung to each other for reasons other than loving each other.

She's probably right.

But I didn't do it. I didn't move in with him. That has to count for something.

"If you won't move in, at least you know you can come and go as you please. You're always welcome here, Rabbit. You're my family. You and Little Rabbit."

He called me and Avery Rabbit and Little Rabbit. He says it reminds him of my calling him White Rabbit at the end of our first date. I never told him that I only called him that because I had forgotten his name.

The embryo took. Blood and urine tests confirmed what Holly intuitively felt. We were going to have another baby. Which meant I had a little less than nine months to tell Jay about the baby, and likely about Holly, and to tell Holly about Jay.

The weight of all of the confessing felt like the world, and I was just an overweight Atlas.

Each time I saw Jay, and maybe in each conversation he and I had, I thought about telling him about the pregnancy. I ran through scenarios in my mind of his possible reactions. Few scenarios ended with me and him still together, and a couple ended with him telling Holly about the relationship. He was—is—vindictive like that.

Then he told me his mother was dying.

Cancer. Not the first time. Doctors don't know how long she has to live.

"Is it terminal?" I asked. Is it terminal; not is she dying.

"We don't know. She's going to fight. Chemo and stuff. We've gone through this before."

I was silent, so he was silent, and then he wasn't silent.

"Is this too much?"

"Your mother having cancer?"

"Yes."

He sounded like he was afraid of my answer.

"We can get through this together."

"I've heard that before," he said, and then he told me about the last time his mother was diagnosed with cancer, and how the man he had been dating had said they'd go through it together. Then, once Jay moved out of the home he shared with this man and into his mother's home, the man said the cancer and the distance were too much.

I hated this man, because he had broken Jay's heart.

"Do you need to be with her?" I asked.

"Not yet," he said, "but I am going to go home for a visit in a few weeks."

"I'm not going anywhere. I take you as is. I'm not scared." His words the night he met Avery, returned.

"Everything will be all right. We'll get through this together."

Kathy is right. Jay and I were—are—shattered, and our pasts have been blasted by the sort of loss that makes even the pretense of normal life impossible. We made the best of what we had been given, and we hoped that someone would understand and love us anyway. Sometimes I wondered if our similarly shattered pasts made each other more attractive than we would have been under different circumstances.

6

Holly driving us home and I'm deleting e-mails and text messages from people concerned about me. My boss had called, as had her boss. They both told me to take off as much time as I needed.

"When I called you out of work, I told your boss where you were," Holly says.

"How did she take it?"

"She just said OK."

I work in health care. St. Elizabeth's reputation precedes itself.

They both know what I likely did to end up there.

I haven't thought about the ramifications of my actions on my place of employment. Jay likely hadn't thought that far either.

If the process server tried to serve me with the restraining order at work, then I'll have even more questions to answer.

I love him but I hate him too.

In Holly's purse, the envelope with the sonogram inside telling us if we are having a boy or a girl.

7

After Jay left to visit his mother, I started imagining what he was doing while he was there. Spending time with her, sure, but also seeing his sister and likely ex-boyfriends. With his sister, he used crystal meth like a fiend. With these ex-boyfriends—well, I didn't like thinking about what he used to do with these exes.

The longer he was gone, the more convinced I became that he was using crystal meth. The more convinced I became, the angrier I became. The angrier I became, the less often I responded to his text messages.

And then one night, five days into his visit, after drinking much more than I should have, I decided to get even with him for all of the crystal meth he was doing and the ex-sex he was having.

Not that I knew for sure he was doing or had done either.

I texted him a picture of the embryo that our fertility doctors gave Holly on the day the embryo was implanted.

"What's this?" he responded.

The picture is gray and murky and indistinguishable from most anything else. Factor in that I texted him a picture of a picture and no wonder he had no idea what he was looking at.

"Holly's pregnant and that's a picture of our baby."

"Why didn't you tell me?"

"This isn't really a decision for you to make."

Poured another drink. Grease on a fire burning out of control and putting at risk everyone who lived nearby.

"How can I be your partner if you don't talk to me about life-changing events that affect both of us if we stay together?"

"Holly and I just found out. I'm telling you now," I told him. "I didn't want to get your hopes up. I didn't want to get my hopes up. I didn't want to interrupt your time with your mother."

Took a step back and waited for the firemen. Didn't want to burn all of it down just yet.

"How is your mother?" I asked.

He waited a few minutes before responding. I expect he wrote and rewrote his response in his measured way, calculating what he should and could and shouldn't and couldn't say.

"We're not done talking about this, but my mother is fine."

Think about that, Jay, the next time you and your sister do crystal or you make out with someone who isn't me, I thought. Think about how my life will move on well without you in it and how you won't get to meet my next child.

"We are done talking about it tonight," I told him. "I'm tired. Holly and Avery are asleep. And this isn't a conversation to really have by text. You're back in a few days. Let's talk about it then."

The day Jay returned, I met him at the train station. I would have met him at the airport, but he didn't want me to miss work. I took him home.

"Look at what mum sent home with me," he said, and he showed me several things from his childhood that his mother had been saving for the right time to give back to him. What Jay didn't say was that this trip wasn't the right time, but might have been the only time that his mother had to give him back the things she had been saving.

"How is she really?" I asked.

"Rabbit," Jay said, starting to cry, "she wants me to be her medical proxy in case she isn't able to make decisions."

"Did you guys talk about her final wishes?"

"A little. But I couldn't really—"

Jay stopped talking. Holding him, while he cried, standing in his bedroom, I felt like his partner.

I rubbed his back.

"I'm here."

"I know. I can't get through this without you."

"Everything will be OK," I said. "I promise."

We didn't talk that day or the next day or even the day after that about the pregnancy. He was busy at work, and I didn't want to bring it up, and by the time the subject came up, Jay made a joke about it.

"I need to meet Holly before she goes into labor," he said.

"You'll meet her before she goes into labor," I said.

8

When we get home, I carry my bag from the hospital upstairs in one hand and I carry Avery with my other arm. He missed me. How do you explain to a not-yet-but-almost three-year-old that his father was in the hospital because he was sad?

How do you explain to anyone something like being sad?

I need to take a shower. The water pressure at the hospital sucked.

I hold open for Holly the door to our home. She thanks me when she gets inside.

I think that Holly and I treating each other civilly, even when we don't feel like treating each other civilly, is something she and I have perfected.

"Are you ready to find out if we're having a boy or a girl?" I ask.

"Yes," she says.

She's waited for me all day; I'm not sure I would have done the same for her.

I pick up Avery. He knows that his mother is pregnant. He knows that we're about to find out if he is getting a brother or a sister.

"We're having a boy," I say, before Holly opens the envelope.

"No, I think we're having a girl," she says.

"What do you think, Avery?"

"Sister," he says. "I'm having a sister."

He and Holly are right. On the back of the sonogram picture is the word GIRL written with a bright yellow highlighter. I reach for Holly, and we hug each other, and she's crying and I'm crying and Avery doesn't know why we're crying but he's touching my face and he says "Daddy sad," and I say "I'm not sad at all."

Inside Holly grows more than just the word GIRL written in yellow highlighter; inside Holly grows an Aurora, the name Holly picked weeks ago, before she knew what I was keeping from her.

While Holly is in the bathroom, I text Jay from her phone: *We're having a girl. I thought you'd want to know.*

I delete the text from her sent texts.

60

After Avery falls asleep, I tell Holly that I need to clean out my car, which is still where I parked it when I got home from the Tobin Bridge the night I decided to jump off of it.

I'm not safe. I don't want to die. Help me, Holly.

Come home, Will. Everything will be OK. Just come home.

I stand outside of my car. I want to unlock the car and begin cleaning it out, but I'm afraid of what I'll find: Ticket stubs and napkins and empty paper cups. CDs made before road trips. Hospital ID bracelets.

A siren in the distance, then the clanging bell of a train. I put everything inside the car into a plastic bag. I bring the bag upstairs and put it on our kitchen table. Holly is sitting in the living room. She looks at me, and at the things I've brought upstairs.

"Do you want some tea?" she asks.

"That would be nice," I say.

We sit together on the couch, as if we hadn't sat on this couch every day for more than a decade. We have run out of things to say to each other.

We have so much to say to each other.

I know I will divide what is in the bag into piles of things to keep and things to somehow get back to Jay.

I know I won't throw anything away. Two kinds of people in the world: Those who keep things and those who don't. I'm a keeper.

I used to tell Jay that all the time.

He'd usually agree that he was too.

Turns out he is more the type of person who throws things away.

I decide to return to work. On my way there, I drive by the store where Jay works, and then I pass the park next to it. He tagged a bench for me there, using a black marker to spell out a message only I would understand: W – I wish you wonder. J.

An author had written the phrase "I wish you wonder" inside a book she signed for Jay. She was his first author. Jay hadn't even known authors went on tour.

"So they're kind of like rock stars?"

"Kind of," I said.

This author wrote "I wish you wonder" inside Jay's book, and he read that sentence dozens of time while I drove us to his apartment after the event. Each time he read the sentence out loud, he changed which word he emphasized.

I wish you wonder. I *WISH* you wonder. I wish *YOU* wonder. I wish you *WONDER*.

He started using this phrase as shorthand for I love you, and then he started using it to say goodbye.

"No one has ever tagged a bench for me," I told him.

"You are everything wonderful and beautiful in my life," he told me. "If you want me to tag others, I will."

I don't think he ever did, but there easily could be another bench out there with a message only I will understand. Breadcrumbs leading Hansel and Gretel to grandmother's house.

I don't know how else to get to work but by driving past the store where Jay works. I park and I wait in my car until I know I will be late. I don't want to answer the questions I'm expecting. I've been gone nearly a week, and on the day I left, I did so with little warning. I obviously had been crying. My boss, despite our differences, didn't question my request to leave.

That was six days ago.

So seven days since I touched and kissed Jay.

You never know when the last time is the last time, not until after.

When I walk into the suite where my office is, a couple of friends ask me if I'm OK, and I say I'm fine and that I need to check my e-mail, and that I have a lot to do, and I'm told that they're here if I need anything, and I'm grateful—of course I'm grateful—but I think people should understand that saying I am sad is all I can say. I am sad should be enough. Don't make me relive everything by asking me what happened.

I am vague, when my boss asks about my missed days, and I am vague about the partial-hospital program, too.

11

I wrote Jay 130, one-page letters during my inpatient stay. I wasn't supposed to, and I had no intention of sending the letters, but I needed to write down everything before I started to forget it all.

I should want to forget.

Like how he washed my back in the shower before he'd wash his hair. Or how he surprised me with a toothbrush to keep at his apartment. Or how he bought diapers for when Avery was there.

In each letter, I explained why I did what I did and why I said what I said and why I didn't say what I didn't say and how much better I could be and how much I loved him and what was happening to me at St.

63

Elizabeth's because, still, he was the one with whom I wanted to share the details about my day.

I just lied. I knew even while writing the letters that I was going to send them to him. He'll read them and understand. He won't want to hear everything from me, not in person, but he'll read the story, separate from me, and he'll think about everything, and he'll know that I'm right.

He and I can—and will—get through this.

I photocopy the letters—can't give him the only copies—and put them in an envelope. I address the envelope to Jay, stamp it, and put it in the outgoing mail.

Details to focus on, each step in the process, instead of focusing on his reaction when he opens his mailbox and sees the envelope there.

And if he doesn't open the envelope, then I will keep trying: Sign language. Carrier pigeon. Smoke signals. Morse code. Sunday morning adverts.

12

After coming out to Holly, and confessing the affair, and after she took off her wedding and engagement rings and told her parents what was going on, I told her that she had to help me win back Jay. That I loved him. That she knew me best, still, and could explain to him in ways I couldn't why I did what I did.

She said no at first, then later, after I again asked, she said she'd think about it. She didn't share the e-mails verbatim with me during my stay at St. Elizabeth's, but only later, when she thought his words wouldn't hurt me.

Holly
There were many things that go into my decision, mostly that I feel extremely violated by Will's actions. I cannot grasp, regardless of the reason or intent—a lot of his actions and this most recent one being the worst. I love Avery and love Will both and I always will, but at this point I think it's best to just part ways. I also kept asking to get to know you more and I wish I had had the chance to do so; I gather this was intentional on Will's part. I was expected to open myself up without walls and I did so, only to be met by wall after wall and a general sense of distrust. I cannot be in a relationship based on conditional trust where I have to fight to prove myself. I wish things could have turned out differently. Let me know if Saturday after 5PM would be an OK time to exchange things.

She wrote him the same day my relationship with him ended. He responded two days later, after I had checked myself into St. Elizabeth's. When Holly replied, she told him what I had done and where I was. He responded to that second email in less than two hours.

Holly
I am at a loss as to what to say and what I can do. This truly upsets me to my core. Has this ever been an issue or happened before? I wanted to say something more to him about the way he acted at the party and the subsequent days. It seemed like he was almost manic—very energized and happy, almost high. When I did ask about his happy mood, his reasoning behind it was that he was finally OK in our relationship, so I didn't push the reason more. However, I do have to say that I think there is something more there, because I've seen his mood swings and often his logic doesn't make sense. I am not sure what a good move on my part would be? I don't want to talk with him and give him hope that we'll get back together. But, I do want to

65

know how he is and if there is truly something I can do that doesn't hurt him more. Or if there's anything I can do to help you? This above all things was never my intent to hurt him like this, and to in turn hurt you and Avery. I never thought that he would react this way, nor do I feel I had many other choices.

Apparent, the difference in Jay's e-mails, even to Holly, Jay's first e-mail more calculated than the second, saying what he thought he needed to say, or what he thought Holly needed to hear, making himself victim and vindicated.

The second e-mail, off the cuff, honest, maybe even proof that he loved me.

Which is why these e-mails hurt. They are buried landmines, waiting to explode, time and again, each reading, the blast zone spreading wider and wider.

And Holly at the epicenter, strong when I couldn't be.

Holly didn't tell me about Jay's initial or subsequent response to her emails when she and Avery visited me at St. Elizabeth's that first night, not until near the end of the visit. A nurse had escorted the three of us to a room the staff uses for meals. Holly sat in one chair; I sat in another. Avery sat in my lap briefly, then wandered around the room. He climbed on chairs, and fell off chairs, and laughed. Each time he fell, he laughed and he picked himself up, and he said "more, more, more."

I didn't know what to say to her, and I don't think she knew what to say to me.

"I fucked it all up."

"Are you talking about with him or about with me?" she asked.

"Both of you, but mainly him."

"I'm not ready to talk more about it."

"I tried so hard to please both of you."

"You certainly fucked that up."

Avery climbed into my lap again, settling his head against my chest. I wrapped my arms around him. I felt like I was holding a shield. Holly couldn't get madder at me while I was holding our son.

"When were you planning to tell me about him?"

"I don't know. Maybe after the baby was born."

"What would you have told me?"

"That Jay and I were in love, and that I was going to move in with him. I would have told you I wanted to get divorced because I wanted to marry him."

"What about the kids?"

"Jay and I talked about having a room for them."

"You wanted them to live with you?"

"No," I said. "Part-time. You and I would have co-parented."

"But you would have had someone to help you co-parent."

"Yes."

"That wouldn't have been fair," she said. "I should go."

"Will you come back tomorrow?"

"Yes, but I'm not going to bring Avery."

I kissed the top of Avery's head, and I handed him to Holly.

"Can I call you?" I asked.

"That's fine," she said. "You shouldn't stay in your room all day. People will think you're depressed."

"I think I am depressed. My heart hurts."

"Does it hurt for him or for me?"

"For him," I said. "I can't mourn the end of my relationship with you while I'm mourning the end of my relationship with him. If I have to do that, I will drown."

So far gone that I stopped thinking about how my words were still hurting Holly. I had already wounded her. I'm gay. I'm in love with someone else. Help me get him back.

Holly strapped Avery into his stroller.

"He wants me to come get your stuff, but I don't really want to," she said. "I wasn't part of the relationship, and I shouldn't be part of its end."

"He wrote?"

"Yes."

"Will you ask Jay if he wants any of the tickets I bought us for upcoming concerts?"

Holly looked at me.

"Please? I won't be able to use the tickets, and they should get used."

"Write down the different concerts, and I'll ask him," she said.

"Thank you," I said. "I'll see you tomorrow."

Holly
You can thank Will for the offer of selling me some of the tickets. However, I don't feel like I would be able to attend any of these events. Do you mind if I ask what actually happened? Did he try to hurt himself? If you don't wish to tell me or he doesn't want me to know, it's understandable. I am fine with exchanging stuff whenever. And if it comes to a point where you still can't see me, we can select a time and I will have what items I have placed on the porch in a few boxes and you can just come by and swap. I don't wish to cause any more pain or inconvenience.

"Did you hear from him?" I asked the next night, when she returned during visiting hours.

"Yes. He wanted to know what you did to yourself."

"What did you tell him?"

"Enough for him to know why you were here."

"I'm sorry you have to talk to him. I wish things were different."

"Me too," she said.

"He hates me."

"I don't think he knows what to feel right now, Will. You hurt him."

"How do I unhurt him?"

"I'm not sure you can. I think you can just work on you and make sure that you don't do this to someone else you love."

Holly

I am sorry for all of this. I've been trying to wrap my mind around why Will would even try to kill himself. I never thought he would do something like that. Even if Will thought it was a viable solution to something, and I can't understand how he would, I assumed he would be thinking of Avery above all. The only time he's even mentioned suicide before was in relation to Avery somehow dying. He said that he wouldn't know how to continue on with his life without Ave. I honestly think there has to be something on a deeper level, although I have no doubt that me breaking up with him must have been a trigger. I really don't know what else to say. I am glad that he didn't go through with it. I still love Will and never want to see him in pain. I am sure though that you would agree it's best if I keep out of the way, as much as I want to call him and talk him through this. The absolute last thing I want for Will is for him to end his life and you can tell him that if you so desire.

Holly's visit during my last night in the psych ward happened in a hallway around the corner from the nurse's station. We weren't allowed to visit in my room. Not like we were going to make out or have sex or anything.

Holly and I watched a woman with a suitcase pushing on the fire escape door. The door was locked. The woman didn't understand why the door wouldn't open. Holly and I looked at each other and tried not to laugh.

"I can tell you loved him, and I'm sorry that that love is gone," Holly said. "You will love again."

"And us?"

"We're going to be OK."

"How do you know?"

"Will," she said, "when have we ever not been OK?"

"I'm sorry," I said.

"I know," Holly said.

She hugged me before she left, which was the first time she had touched me since I had told her about Jay.

Had you watched this scene, there in the hospital, you wouldn't have guessed that I had spectacularly blown apart our world. Or maybe you would have guessed, because mixed in with the worry and the uncertainty was a little relief. No need to tap dance around why we no longer connected.

The biggest betrayal, probably, had you been watching this scene unfold in the hospital, was I thought that salvaging my friendship with Holly was secondary to getting back together with Jay.

I Statements

1

I've returned to St. Elizabeth's for the second day of the partial-hospital program. I'm waiting for Erin and the intern to arrive. Chris, a man I met on Monday who says he's there for help dealing with his anxiety, is sitting at the head of the large table (which is really two smaller square tables pushed against each other). He nods at me when I walk in, but doesn't say anything. He looks like a football player, the kind who likely made high school hell for gay kids.

Erin arrives, and behind her walks the intern. I don't remember her name.

Erin looks at me and Chris. She smiles. Encouraging, Erin's smile.

"Do you like yourself?"

Erin does not pose the question as much as she attacks with it. Or that's how her question feels.

No one responds. Who likes feeling attacked so early in the morning? I'm still on my first cup of coffee. Decaf, since Kathy asked me to cut out all stimulants until we see how effective the Lamictal is and if there are side effects.

But if my skin starts to fall off, I told her, I'm going to need something a bit stronger than Folgers Decaf.

"Let's try something else," Erin says. "When you like yourself, you make better choices. You choose to spend time with positive people. You surround yourself with healthy people. Do you guys think you have surrounded yourself with healthy people?"

"No," I say, and Chris shakes his head. Chris. Brown hair. Brown eyes. Glasses. He's wearing a T-shirt with the logo of the Patriots on it. Cut-off shorts. The hair on his legs is black, curly, kind of sparse. His legs are tan as are his arms. Chris. The guy with anxiety who probably played high school football and ate fags for breakfast.

"You choose the type of person you are. You choose the type of person you have in your life," Erin says. "Feel better about yourself, and you'll make better choices."

Erin talks in slogans. Most of the people who work at St. Elizabeth's talk in slogans.

I hate slogans.

The poster of the kitten in the tree, holding on to a branch with one paw, and the words *Hang In There* or something similarly cheery and hopeful beneath.

Confession: Sometimes I've thought about the kitten's reaction if I was there in that moment with a saw, separating branch from tree.

Down will come kitty, inspirational slogan and all.

The Lamictal should slow my mind, according to the author of the drug's Wikipedia page. The information there is the same information Kathy told me. Except in the author's use of "how my mind will learn to stay quiet."

Like my mind has a mouth or something.

Took the first pill yesterday, and I took the second pill today. Twenty-five milligrams a day for seven days. Then 50 milligrams a day for seven days. Each week for four weeks, upping the dose by 25 milligrams. At 100 milligrams a day, said Kathy, she and I would decide if we're going to stop there or if I should titrate to a higher dosage.

Erin saying my name in a way that makes me think she's said it once or twice already.

I look at her, to show her that I'm listening.

"What are you grateful for?"

Seriously? Let's go back to if I like myself. That's easier to answer than what I'm grateful for.

"Grateful for?" I repeat.

"Grateful for," she says.

"I'm not dead."

"What else," she prompts.

"I've had the same partner for more than 12 years who hasn't given up on me, even though she likely should have. I have a son who loves me. I'm going to soon have a daughter. I have a job with enough flexibility that I can spend all day here."

I am in love with a man named Jay who claims he wants to marry me.

I am in love with a man named Jay who claimed he wanted to marry me. Past tense. Likely has already forgotten the ring that was too large for his ring finger anyway.

"And how often do you think about the things that are going well in your life?"

"Not very often."

"Most of us don't," Erin says. "Easier thinking about the bad stuff than the good, right?"

"Yes," Chris says.

"Change that thinking. Incorporate gratitude into your daily life. Be grateful for the good parts and the bad parts. Sometimes, the bad parts turn out to be something good. You'll be happier."

Hold on, Erin, I think. Bad parts turning out to be the good parts? Unlikely. Tell me how losing Jay will benefit me in the long run? I wanted to marry him. I wanted to raise children with him. We had so many plans— adventures to have, pictures to find in clouds, balloons to fill with helium, houses to fly.

"And you should focus less on what you think is negative in your life and more on the positive," Erin says.

Chris, the intern, and I just look at Erin.

"If you think about bad things long after the thing has ended, then you're living in your museum," Erin says. "We all have these museums. Instead of storing happy moments and fun times, we store the bad things that have happened. Will, tell us about your museum. Tell us about the art on the walls, the moments you know you shouldn't think about but do anyway."

2

In order to date Jay, I had to agree to some ground rules about how our relationship couldn't end. I couldn't end our relationship via a text message or during a phone call, and before we for-good ended the relationship, we had to have seven knockdown, drag-out fights. Those were his terms. He outlined them for me immediately after asking me if I wanted to date it out with him. I agreed to his terms, though I wondered about what must have happened to Jay for him to raise his concern at the beginning of our relationship about its end.

His rules of life didn't end at how his relationships couldn't end. He didn't talk to exes. Refused to hold down more than one job at a time, even when he could have used the extra income. Preferred the bus to the train, but would take the train if he had to. Deleted playlists from his iTunes after listening to them for a week. Talked to his mother at least three times a week, which became daily once her cancer returned. All of these rules, to keep things straight in his head, he said.

Only now can I see that these rules were his way of trying to control what he could about his out-of-control life. But when you're in the spinning teacup, and the ride won't slow down, you don't look far below the surface. Jay had rules; I agreed to the ones that affected me.

And for a while, we didn't argue. But then the things we weren't saying to each other begin to pile up. His mother, and what her cancer meant to his relationship with me and to Boston. My wife, about whom he still knew nothing. His pot use, becoming something he used every day, sometimes more than once a day. My second child, who would be boy or girl, healthy or not, but part of my life all the same; I never felt like he and I truly sorted out my decision not to tell him that Holly and I were trying again.

Alone in my teacup, faster and faster it went until I had to shut my eyes to keep everything un-topsy-turvy.

The nights Jay asked me not to come over because he was going to be using. The friends of mine Jay hadn't met, which were all of my friends, since no one knew the extent of my relationship with Jay. How he hadn't met Holly, or wasn't even allowed in my home when she was around. How much I disliked his closest friends.

That was clear, though he and I avoided talking about it. He gave me all of the time he could—all of the time he didn't spend with his friends.

His usual refrain, when he could tell that his making plans to use had upset me: It's you I love best.

The things we didn't say but carried were there in all of the things we said.

I often talked to Jay in my head, trying out different topics of conversation, especially topics I knew would upset him. Like how he should stop using, or use less. Or how I thought a couple of his close friends were secretly in love with him.

Making mountains out of molehills, as one of my grandmothers often said.

These conversation monologues never ended well.

Convinced that Jay's interest in me was waning—though my only real proof was how frequently he asked for time away so he could use—I started giving him reasons to stay with me. I'd pay when we ate out, or I'd pick up something I knew he wanted but that he couldn't afford. One weekend, after Holly and I went through some boxes in our attic and put together a pile of things to get rid of, I offered several things to Jay that I knew he could use: a lamp, some picture-hanging wire, a shelving unit, some hangers, and two picture frames.

I told Jay I'd bring everything over one night when Holly was at her book club, and after she left, I put everything in my car, and then put Avery in his car seat. Dual purpose for the visit: Jay got a few things that he wanted, and he'd get time with Avery, something he'd lose if our relationship ended.

Avery was overtired and crying. I tilted the rearview mirror so I could watch him, and no matter how I contorted my face, he wouldn't stop crying. I expected he would settle down, once we were in Jay's room, and eventually fall asleep. When we got to Jay's apartment, he was outside waiting, and I figured he would help me bring up everything, and then we'd come back for Avery, who was still crying. Jay lived in a safe enough neighborhood, and if he and I took up everything, we could do it in one trip. But doing so would mean leaving Avery in the car.

I was pulling things out of the trunk, and I could hear Jay consoling Avery. Under different circumstances, Jay comforting Avery would have been almost sexy, in an I'm-meant-to-be-with-you kind of way, but under these circumstances, it just made me angry that Jay wasn't helping me.

Jay carried in Avery, and I carried in everything else, walking several feet behind Jay. As what I was carrying shifted in my arms and hands, I tried to hold everything, but I couldn't. A hanger dropped, then the roll of picture wire, then I was holding the lamp by its cord, and then I wasn't holding anything. The light bulb in the lamp broke, when it hit the ground.

"Are you OK?" Jay asked. He had stopped at the steps leading into his apartment building. Avery's eyes were half-open, his head burrowed into Jay's shoulder.

"No," I said. "I am not OK."

I picked up everything, walked past Jay and Avery, dropped everything in the foyer of the apartment building, and went back outside. Jay hadn't moved.

"Give me my son," I said.

"What?" he asked.

"Give me my son."

When Jay didn't hand me Avery, I took him from Jay. Avery woke up, looked around, and went back to sleep. The top of his head smelled like Jay's lotion.

"Will," Jay said, questioning, maybe even surprised.

I left him there, and took Avery home. I was mad at myself for dropping everything, but instead of blaming myself for not making two trips, I blamed Jay for not helping me. By the time I got home, Avery was asleep. I wasn't angry anymore, and I knew I needed to apologize.

"You reminded me of my father," Jay said, when I called him. I was parked outside of my condo. Holly was still at book club. Avery was snoring. "He would throw things when he got mad."

"But I didn't throw anything. I couldn't carry everything. One thing fell, and then another, and I just let it all fall so I could pick everything back up and start again. I was just angry."

"I will not be in a relationship with someone who cannot handle their anger better."

"I'm sorry," I said.

"I don't like thinking that you can take Avery away, and I don't have a say."

"I didn't want to fight with you in front of him."

"But you took him without regard for my feelings," Jay said. "You took him from me and you left. You can always do that."

"He's my son," I said. I looked in the rearview mirror at Avery. Still, so much of Holly in the way my son looks and acts.

"You say he's our son," Jay countered.

He was right. And I had been wrong.

"I'm sorry I took him from you," I said. "I will not do that again."

"I'm sorry, too."

The night I met Brett, Jay's best friend, he came over unannounced to see if Jay wanted to go to a bar. I was making Jay sushi, had just added sushi rice to a pot of boiling water, and in walked Brett. Jay introduced us, and Brett moonwalked across the kitchen floor before lightly punching my shoulder.

"What are you making?" he asked.

"Sushi," I said.

Then, I wanted Brett to like me, since Jay had said how close they were.

"Looks like you're using too much water," he said, before dancing his way back to the side of the kitchen where Jay was drinking a beer.

"Have you made sushi before?" I asked. Because I had. Dozens of times. And while I may not always measure when I cook, I know enough to know how much water to put in a pot that will then be used to cook rice.

"No," Brett said.

"Then how do you know I'm using too much water?"

"Just looks like you are."

He invited Jay out, and Jay said that he and I had plans.

"You don't mind, do you, if we go out?" Brett asked.

"If that's what Jay wants to do," I said.

"I'm hanging out with Will tonight," Jay said. "But you're not staying over, right?" he asked me.

"No," I said.

"Brett, why don't I call you when Will leaves, and if you're up, you can come back."

Brett agreed, left, and came back after I left. The two of them smoked a lot of weed, Jay told me the next night.

"Don't mind him," Jay said. "That's just who he is."

Jay's friends, the ones I met, said the same thing and that I would like him if I gave him a chance.

One night, Jay asked me to pick him up at work around midnight, which I did. I took him home and even though I had to be up with Avery in a few hours, I went upstairs with Jay. I wanted to hang out. I wanted to hear about his day. I wanted to get laid.

We were having sex when Brett texted. He was downstairs and wanted to get some weed from Jay. Jay's phone lights up when he gets a text message. We both saw the message come in, and then he stopped what he was doing, which stopped what I was doing, and he reached for his phone. He read his message and then got out of bed, put on pants, and went downstairs.

I thought about getting dressed, but we hadn't finished, and I wanted to finish.

I was expecting him to pack a bowl and smoke in our post-coital conversation, but he surprised me.

"Brett was hoping you were going home soon," Jay said. "He wants to smoke with me. Do you mind?"

I should have said that I minded.

But I told him that I didn't mind. I went to the bathroom, put on my clothes, and I left.

Brett was still parked downstairs. I waved at him from my car, and then I drove home.

The next morning, I took Avery to the Charles River. While we were there, Jay texted twice to see what we were doing. I didn't respond until later that evening, and I played off my absence during the day. When he didn't respond, I called. The sound of his voice when he said hello told me that he had decided to end our relationship.

"You want to break up," I said.

He paused—at least he paused—before he said yes.

Should have seen it as a clean exit. Holly would never know, and I'd likely never run into Jay or his friends. I could go back to how things had been before I met Jay.

Except I didn't want to go back to how things had been.

"Why? What did I do?"

"It's a lot of things," Jay said. "You didn't tell me about the baby. You won't let me spend time with Holly. You have all these walls up, and you're not letting me in."

I was in my car, at a red light. Avery was home with Holly. If I turned to the right, I'd be home in a few minutes. If I turned to the left, I could be at Jay's apartment in less than fifteen minutes.

I did not hang up, and Jay did not hang up, but we did not say anything. I could hear him breathing, and I was trying not to think that this phone call would be the last time he and I were on the phone together.

Those monologue conversations he and I shared in my head were all about to happen.

Despite how often I prepared, I knew I wasn't ready.

"Why haven't you said any of this before?" I finally asked.

"I have, Will," he said. "And last night, I ended up on the floor crying because I don't understand why you won't let me in, and I don't want to cry anymore. You haven't introduced me to your friends. You haven't made me part of your life, and I've given you full access to everything. I don't understand why you won't let me in."

You were getting high last night, I thought. You and Brett. You stopped having sex with me so you could give Brett some weed. You asked me to go home after we were done having sex.

81

Any of those statements would have ended the conversation and our relationship, which still wasn't over; saying he wanted to end it wasn't the same as actually ending it.

"In my head, I gave you a time frame in which to introduce me to Holly. The time is up. I don't understand why I haven't met her. She's the mother of your child, and she's carrying your second child. I'm your partner, and I haven't met her, and I don't know why. I gave you keys to my apartment, but I've barely been in your home. I asked you to move in with me, because I want you to move in with me, and you don't have a good enough reason why you won't do it."

Lights changing red to green to yellow and signs that say stop and yield and blind alley. One-way roads and four-way stops and the different ways you can get from my house to Jay's house and if he and I broke up I'd never be able to go back to the town where he lives because what if we ran into each other. Worse, what if I ran into him and his new boyfriend?

I told him I was there when I got to his apartment.

"OK," Jay said. He hung up.

He was in his bed. I sat in the chair at his computer desk. He and I were in the same positions we had been the night we met. I knew he was right. I hadn't been fair. I couldn't give him the access he wanted. But I had offered him the access I could. Avery. My second child. As soon as we could begin forever.

"I can't just tell Holly that I've met someone else, and I'm going to move in with him, and I love him. She's my family. She's the mother of my children. I told you I would introduce the two of you when the time is right. I want to spend my life with you, Jay, but I need time to figure out how to make it all work."

"I don't want to wait," Jay said. "I love you. I'm in love with you. I want that life, and I want that life now."

"I can't do that," I said.

Jay had taken down all of the pictures he had put up of me and of Avery, and had put Avery's toys and clothes into a plastic bag. Nothing left to indicate that he was in a relationship or that he loved me.

My heart ached. My throat was dry. Swallowing was difficult, as was talking. If Jay left me, then I'd be stuck going back to a life I no longer wanted. And if Jay left me, then I'd be stuck waiting for someone like him to again pick me. And if Jay left me, then something must be wrong with me.

I waited for him to say that he was no longer interested in dating it out. That we had reached the end of our experiment and that our alchemical arrangement was over, gold becoming lead once again.

"This is my life," I said. "It's messy and a lot, and I know it's a lot, but you said you took me as is, and I trusted you meant as is when you said it."

"I did," he said.

Past tense.

"Do you want me to go?"

Jay shook his head no. I took off my shoes, got into bed with him.

"You don't give me enough time, Rabbit. I need more than what you're giving. I want whole nights. I want mornings. I want full access."

"I'm giving you what I can."

He was crying.

"I don't want to have to talk you into staying with me. Either you want to or you don't want to," I said.

I got out of bed.

"Don't go," Jay said.

"Why not?"

"Because I love you."

I got back into his bed.

"I haven't loved anyone like I love you," he said. "I don't want to lose you."

"I don't want to lose you either."

And we fit those jagged pieces together. Not fit as much as smashed.

I was trying to hold together something that had been broken, and more than being broken, something that had started out broken. He, and me, and he with me, and all of the ways I was deceiving him, and the ways he unintentionally hurt me on the nights he didn't want me around. All of it broken. But if my relationship with Holly had taught me anything, it was how to hold together something that is broken.

"What would you have done if this had turned out differently?" I asked. "What if we had not decided to stay together?"

"I had bought a new lock for the front door. It's in the living room. I would have asked you to give me back my keys, and if you wouldn't have, I would have changed the locks."

"If you had asked for your keys back, I would have given them to you. If you don't want me around, just tell me. You don't have to change your locks. I'm not like your other exes."

Because one had, Jay had told me, refused to return keys and even waited for Jay to come home from work one night. This ex is the reason why Jay has rules about not talking to exes.

"I just like being prepared," Jay said.

4

"Those are perfect examples of the types of things we keep in our museums," Erin says. "You can't change what happened. You can't go back and say or do things differently. But you can't stop thinking about any of the things either."

"But I want to," I say. "If I could go back and just do things differently."

"Nothing would have changed," Erin says.

"If I had been honest with him from the beginning, I think he and I would have had a chance."

Those letters I mailed yesterday when I was at work, written in ink while I was stuck in a room with a man who brought 30 pairs of underwear with him, written until I had the start of blisters on the skin separating thumb from index finger on my right hand. Those letters are on their way to his apartment right now. Will likely get there sometime after the group breaks for lunch.

"You have to let it all go," Erin says.

"OK," I say.

She knows I don't mean OK.

"What's stopping you?"

"If I stop thinking about making things better with Jay, then I have to accept that I have no one."

"A lot of us feel like we can't be alone, so we hang on to someone because the alternative is no one, and no one wants to think that they don't deserve to be with someone. But you can't spend time thinking about the things you can't change. Think about the things you can change, like how you and Holly are going to raise your children going forward. You can do something about that."

5

He doesn't text or call. All night I wait for some sign, and when I can't fall asleep, I take an Ambien, another prescription from Kathy that she hopes I no longer need by the time the partial-hospital program ends. Hadn't slept well before St. Elizabeth's, and haven't slept well since. My brain and the Lamictal circling each other, taking the other's measure. I want the Lamictal to win.

Jay e-mails at 5:40 a.m. I hear my phone register the received message, and I check. He titled the e-mail *My Final Song* and attached an mp3 to the e-mail, but the message is empty.

I don't need to download the song to know what the song is. Jay had told me months ago the name of the song he considered ours, and he also told me the song he thought would represent our relationship at its end.

A couple of hours later, Holly gets a text message from Jay. Holly and Avery are still asleep, and I'm awake drinking coffee, and I'm curious about who is texting her so early, so I check.

"I didn't know you are or were married. Will lied about everything. I'm not angry anymore, and I forgive him, but I can't go with him on the path he's on. I will always love Will and Avery both."

I take a screenshot of the text message, e-mail it to myself, and then delete the text, the picture, and the sent e-mail from Holly's phone. When I tell Holly about hearing from Jay, I leave out the text message part.

"You're not going to listen to the song?"

"No."

"So, what are your plans?" Holly asks.

"About moving out? About our divorce? About what?"

"All of it, really, but you can date if you want to. Don't feel like you can't date."

"I won't be ready to date for a long time," I say.

"Well, don't fall in love. I don't want any plans we make about our future to be jeopardized because you think you're in love."

6

During the third session of the partial-hospital program, Erin suggests I delete the photos of Jay and his text messages from my phone.

"You need to delete his phone number, too."

"I deleted it the day we broke up."

I hadn't. And didn't want to.

I haven't deleted his last voicemail, left about two weeks ago, telling me how much he loves me, either.

I can listen to him when I want to.

"Change doesn't have to be negative," Erin says. "What makes change negative is how we view situations. Our thoughts increase negative change. Using loaded words can increase fear and anxiety regarding change. What kind of loaded words do you use?"

"That I fucked up my life."

Erin nods.

"What else?"

"That I hurt the people I care about the most. That I had no right to hurt either of them. That I missed out on a lot of my son's life this year because I wasn't always around. That I'm going to make these mistakes again. That I'm never going to fall in love again. That I'm never going to not feel what I feel."

"Sometimes change means having no control over a situation," she says. "You don't have control over this situation. So let go. Let go of the guilt. Let go of the baggage. Letting go means not beating yourself up because of it. Letting go means telling the voices in your head that tell you that you're not good enough or that you won't love again or that you fucked up to be quiet and let you live."

You'll never love again. You're nothing without me.

More things from Jay that I can't delete.

7

Jay texted one afternoon that he had thrown up twice, felt like he was going to black out, and was getting a ride home from work. I was at work, too.

"Can I do anything?" I responded.

"No, I'm just going home to sleep."

When I went over to his apartment that night, he confessed a history of childhood migraines, but that he hadn't had a migraine in several years.

"I've had a headache for the last couple of days, but today it was just like I was a kid again," he said.

"Should I be worried?" I asked.

"I'll be fine."

Jay slept for days, called out of work until he used all of his sick days, took a short-term leave of absence, saw several doctors, and covered his windows with blankets so that his bedroom was always dark. I brought him food, took him to his doctor, and had his prescriptions filled.

"I'm going to list you as my emergency medical contact," Jay said. "My mother has been, but she can't really do anything from Illinois."

On a Wednesday when he was still on a short-term leave of absence from work, he texted to let me know he needed me to come get him and take him to the hospital.

Wednesdays are my busiest day at work. I have three meetings in the morning, then two more in the afternoon. Leaving on a Wednesday without notice would not be easy to do, but I thought I could do it between my morning and afternoon meetings.

"I can't," I responded. "But I'll come when I can."

"Don't bother," he said, and he stopped responding to my efforts to reach him.

I couldn't focus during my meetings. Later during the day, Jay texted: I can't get to the doctor on my own. Can you take me now?

"Of course," I say. "Whatever you need."

I came for him, dropped him at the hospital, and told him I'd pick him up after work. After I picked him up, I took him home, helped him get settled, and told him to call that night if he needed anything.

Three more days passed, and Jay's doctors couldn't diagnose what was causing Jay's migraines. Medications were tried and discarded. Four, five, six bottles of pills on Jay's bookshelf, none of which eased his pain.

The migraines began two weeks before Father's Day, and on Father's Day, Jay told me he was in too much pain to do anything but stay in bed. I didn't try to persuade him to change his mind. I told him what I'd been telling him for weeks: Everything will be fine.

I took Avery to a store, bought Jay a Father's Day card, helped Avery sign his name to it, and put inside the card several photographs of me and Avery that we had taken at a photo booth.

I drove to Jay's apartment. Avery was in the backseat repeating Jay's name. At a red light, I saw someone in the distance walking in my direction. This someone looked like Jay, but couldn't be Jay, I thought, since Jay had difficulties taking showers with any lights on.

But the man walking on the sidewalk was Jay.

I pulled my car to the side of the road near Jay.

He walked past my car.

I rolled down my window.

"Where are you going?" I said. "Get in."

Jay shook his head no and kept walking.

I drove to the next block, turned down that street, circled the block, and pulled back alongside Jay.

"Go away," he said, still not looking at me.

Avery in the backseat: "Jay. Jay. Jay."

"Leave me alone. I want to go to the doctor in peace," Jay said.

"Let me take you," I said.

"No."

"What happened?" I asked.

And Jay tilted back his head and screamed. He gripped his head with his hands. I thought he was about to collapse. Cars behind me honked, then swerved to pass.

Jay stood on the side of the road.

Avery calling from the backseat: "Jay. Jay. Jay."

The Father's Day card was in the passenger seat of my car.

The passenger side window was open.

Jay standing on a sidewalk, and his emergency medical contact offering to help in what might be an emergency.

I pulled into a nearby parking lot.

"I'll be right back, Avery," I said. And I left him there, locked in my car, windows rolled down. I ran to Jay, watching Jay walk away from me. His back, the curve of his spine, the miles of skin I had touched and knew. Watching it leave me. Not even a look back to see what was behind him.

Objects in your rear-view mirror are closer than they appear.

I'm here. Stop and let me help you. Stop and explain all of this to me.

Tell me what I did. Tell me how I can fix it.

"What are you doing?" I said to Jay, when I caught up to him. "Talk to me."

"Leave me alone. I can't depend on you to be there for me. You failed me when I needed you. If I had been Holly or Avery, you would have left work without a second thought. You would have been there for them. I am your family, Rabbit, and you were not there for me. I can't trust you to be there for me. You need to go home and forget me."

"I wouldn't have left work for Holly. She wouldn't have asked me to leave work for her. As for Avery, of course I would leave work for him. He's my son."

I followed Jay the length of a city block, but I couldn't leave Avery alone for any longer. I ran to my car, drove to another parking lot, this one closer to where Jay was, and I parked.

"Daddy, what's wrong with Jay?" Avery asked.

"Hold on, baby," I said.

"Let me take you to the doctor," I said to Jay, when I reached him again. "You shouldn't be outside."

"You're doing this to me, you know."

"What?" I asked.

"I was talking to my sister last night, and she suggested that these migraines are because of you, and I was thinking about it, and I think she's right."

"I am not causing your migraines."

"Go home. I need a partner who prioritizes me. And I can find him. You know everyone tells me I'm beautiful. I have my pick of guys. Do you know how many people I work with who tell me that they will have a baby with me? I don't need you. I can move on. You will never find someone who is as good to you as I am."

Jay was screaming.

Avery, still in my car, had started to cry.

"You got lucky when you found me. I was willing to take on your son, and then when you got someone pregnant without telling me about it first, I was willing to take on your other child. There is no one else out there who will take you and your two children. You will not find someone else like me."

"I'm your family," I said. "I cannot unpick you."

"No more," he said. "We are not family."

Jay walked away from me.

"Fine."

I reached into my pocket, pulled out my keys, and I took the keys to his apartment off my ring. "Take these back," I said, and I handed the keys to him.

He took the keys and put them in his pocket.

We were standing outside of his doctor's office. I didn't know what else to say. I felt like I had been gutted, that my heart was gone. My mouth and throat and lips dry. "Can't we talk about this?" I said, one last appeal.

"Just let me go to the doctor."

He walked away from me, and I walked back to my car. A police car pulled into the parking lot, and I thought that someone must have called the police.

"Where's Jay?" Avery asked.

"He's sick."

I didn't elaborate. Avery wouldn't understand.

I didn't fully understand.

The Father's Day card in the passenger seat.

At a red light, halfway between Jay's apartment and my home, I opened the card and I took out the pictures of me and Avery. I put the card back inside the envelope. At the next red light, I began to rip the card. Three red lights later, the card was pieces of red and white paper.

I unrolled my window.

I picked up some of the pieces, held my hand outside the window, and I let the wind take the pieces of the card. Some of the pieces fell to the ground immediately; others took flight.

I texted Jay. I told him that I was sorry for disappointing him, that I loved him, that I was there for him, that he was my family, that I was scared, and that I would never let him down again.

"Let me deal with this," he responded. "I'll call you later."

A reprieve. Still not telling me that we were over.

"I'm sorry," he said, when he called later. "I was scared. I'm tired of my head hurting. I need it to stop, Rabbit."

"I know, Horse."

My decision to nickname Jay "Horse" must have meant something at the time, but I can't remember now why I chose it as his nickname.

"I fucked up," he said. "I wasn't sure if you would pick up the phone for me."

"I'll always pick up the phone for you."

"You know what, Will, I mean, after that whole lovely charade, I kind of looked back on it and was like, Jesus Christ, where do we go from here. Is that something we're going to be able to laugh at? I mean, how can you—I mean, I relived the things I said, and I watched in my mind the way we must have looked. I believe we stopped in four parking lots. But thank you for that. Whatever that was, thank you."

"I didn't do anything I didn't want to do."

"Rabbit, you should revel in all of this. You have the ability to make me want to stay. You know me. You know where everything comes from, when it happens. You have that power. No one else has had it."

"I don't know if power is the word. I have an awareness. I can recognize it."

"I told you that I took you and Avery as is. I didn't say you wouldn't have to come after me. And as unpleasant as that was, it's nice to know that we have a real relationship, where things aren't always perfect. Because I think we do. Everything seems to fall into place a lot of the time, and it's kind of nice to know that we can still fuck up a little bit. You know? And we do it so well together. We do both sides really well."

"It's nice to hear you say you love me," I said.

"Do I not say it often?"

"You do."

"Good. I don't time it. I haven't been keeping track. I know for a while there I felt I was saying I love you a lot, and I thought, maybe I'm saying I love you too much. If there's such a thing, I don't want to wear it out."

"Like you said, everyone who comes into contact with you thinks you're beautiful. You were very clear."

"And you're my it. So I can't say there's much choice in that. It's taken me this long, and I've gone through so much to get here to be with you, aside from some ranting on the side of the road, I mean, why would I throw it all away and never find happiness."

"You could find it," I said.

"You think we could? You think you could walk away from me, and you're going to find something equal to this or better? Haven't you said that you can't see your life without me in it?"

"Yes, but I could find something different."

"Usually when you leave something good," he said, "you should have an upgrade in mind."

He told me what the doctors had told him, more uncertainty, and promises that a cure, or at least an explanation, was coming.

"You're still my emergency medical contact. Is that OK?"

"Of course," I said. "That's who I am."

The next time I saw him, he gave me back the keys to his apartment.

"Never take them off your key ring again," he said.

A few days after, the doctors found a cluster of cells in Jay's head. These cells, the doctors said, were causing the migraines. The doctors neither knew what caused the clusters to form nor what they could do to remove the cluster. They prescribed a different medication, which slowly began to work.

I used to think he kept the medication that didn't work, still in their opaque orange bottles, as a reminder that sometimes you have to try several things before you find something that works. Now I know better.

8

Erin is talking, and has been talking, and I have not been listening. She stops talking and looks at me.

"I'm sorry," I say. "I wasn't listening."

"Is your life tough?" Erin asks.

"I think I make it tougher than it needs to be."

"How is your life tough?"

"I have a son who needs a lot of attention and time."

"How else is your life tough?"

"I fell in love with someone who isn't my wife. I decided to leave my wife for this man. I decided that I was ready to be openly gay. I decided I was responsible for getting him sober. I decided getting him sober was worth losing him, if, in the end, he realized what his addiction was doing to someone he claimed to love."

Kathy told me I needed to take responsibility for my actions.

"Did it work?"

"No. I feel like I wasted the entire year. I feel like I abandoned Holly. I feel like I abandoned myself a little."

We're told to use I statements when talking about our problems.

"Good. Now, let it go. You made mistakes. You're coping with them. You think you did a terrible thing, but you're not a terrible person."

Things. Terrible things, I think.

"Will, forgive yourself."

I'm quiet.

"Will," she says, "say *I forgive myself.*"

"I forgive myself."

"Again, Will."

"I forgive myself."

"Accepting your emotions doesn't mean letting your emotions control you. Accepting your emotions means feeling what you feel. Don't resist what you feel. Don't judge your feelings. Don't judge yourself for having these feelings. Don't act on the emotion. Falling out of love isn't easy. You didn't fall in love with him in a day or even a week. Why would you expect falling out of love to be easy? You're starting a new life, and these first few steps are going to hurt. But you need to move forward. You can't hang out here in limbo."

The Party at the End of the World

1

Before Jay and I had lunch on the day I turned 33, he asked me to open my present. I opened the box, read the note inside that said *Wear Me*, and found, underneath a layer of cotton, a key.

It was the key to his childhood bedroom. The key was on a chain. He had been wearing it around his neck on a chain, and now he was giving it to me.

He took the chain from me, and he clasped it around my neck.

"I love it."

"I hope so, because you'll be wearing it forever," he said.

"I can do that," I said, wondering how I would explain it to Holly, because of course she would ask me where I had gotten the key and why was I wearing it. In the time it took me to think that I needed a clever cover story, I realized I would just tell her that I had found the key at a yard sale, thought it was kind of cool, and had decided to wear it on a chain.

"You don't understand. When we get married, I want to melt the key and use it to make your ring. You will wear my past on your finger as a symbol of our future and life together."

"Our bands won't match," I said.

"I don't care. I want you to have my past. I want you to have my future. You have it all, Rabbit. You know that."

"So are we engaged?" I asked.

Being engaged to Jay, despite already being married, didn't seem as impossible then as it does today.

"Not yet," he said, "but I'll let you know."

With the key on its chain around my neck, I started tempting fate. I stepped on every sidewalk crack. I held his hand and kissed him in public. We ventured out to places where someone who knew Holly might have been. And one evening when we ran into someone who attends book group with Holly, I was vague about how I knew Jay. After, he asked if I wasn't out to this woman, and I said no, not really. And he said that I likely was now, since you can tell when two guys are friends and when they're more than friends.

Jay and I started talking about our future using words like when and soon.

"Our home," Jay often said, probably as besotted with the idea of us being engaged as I was, "will have two stories."

"I want a library, and the kids need a room. Probably separate rooms."

"I want windows in the bathroom and a fenced-in backyard. And a dog."

"A dog?" I asked. "I've never owned a dog."

"A big dog. And two of those," Jay said, pointing to a pair of entwined weeping willows abutting the Charles River.

"And a fire escape, because you like fire escapes," I said. And after putting the kids to bed, on the nights Jay and I had the kids, he and I would sit on that fire escape, drinking tea, counting stars.

"I want a garden," he said. "Vegetables. Flowers."

"I do not have a green thumb," I said.

"I do."

His occasional attempts at husbandry—at tending to tomatoes until we could eat them, for example, or nurturing plants in his office—indicated, to me, his inherent belief in the future. He just didn't know how much tending to I needed.

We'd walk around the Charles River on Saturdays and sometimes Sundays. Jay and Avery would wander near the water's edge. They'd look for sticks and they would scare away ducks. Jay would pick up Avery and spin around.

Avery learned that when he wanted out of his stroller, Jay gave in more often than I did.

"Out," Avery would say, each time we crossed the Massachusetts Avenue bridge.

"Should we let him out?" Jay asked.

"You know I'm not comfortable with that. What would we do if he fell in? I can't swim. I can't get him."

"Rabbit, you won't have to jump in after him because I will jump in after him, and I will not be able to save both of you at the same time," Jay said. "My job is to keep both of you safe, and you need to let me do that."

"You know," I said, "if anything ever happens to Avery, if he would die, I'm not sure I could keep living. I think I would kill myself."

2

I should take comfort in knowing that how my relationship with Jay ended is not the worst way that one of his relationships has ended.

After breaking up with one man, Jay drained the water from his waterbed and left it outside for the man to reclaim. Another man, when he asked for Jay to give back a bracelet, was told that he could have the bracelet, if he felt like looking along the interstate, somewhere along a specific ten-mile stretch of land.

One man cheated on Jay, but when Jay found out, said that he was only doing it for the money and that the sex meant nothing. Getting even with him, Jay said, meant fucking his best friend. Which he did. Twice.

Someone before me, a man named Juan, didn't want to use drugs with Jay. This was when Jay was using crystal and coke and ecstasy, anything he could get, actually. But Juan wasn't going to break up with Jay, so when Jay ended the relationship, Juan kind of broke. He called and texted and would show up outside of Jay's apartment. Sometimes Jay talked to him; other times, Jay ignored him.

Jay said he regretted the end of this relationship more than the ends of any other relationship.

Men that Jay wished he hadn't let fuck him, and men that Jay regretted fucking, and men who wanted more from Jay than he wanted to give, and men who made and broke promises. A married man. A man who wanted an open relationship. Each of these men, Jay said, links on a chain connecting him to me. Break one of these links, and he and I never would have met.

Which meant I should be thankful for Reggie, the guy who introduced Jay to crystal.

Reggie's house was wired with video cameras. He always knew who was standing outside his front door. There were cameras inside too. He was a dealer, or maybe he was just a heavy user. I think Jay and he lived together, and I think Reggie hit Jay. And thanks to Reggie's connections, which soon became Jay's connections, when that relationship imploded, as Jay's relationships did, Jay knew who to ask when he wanted to use.

"That was my bad drug phase," he said, the night he told me about his ex-boyfriends. "That was the one where when I stopped using, I would have dreams, and in my dreams I would be high, and when I woke up, I couldn't believe that I hadn't actually been high. And for about two years after that, I would have times when things would get rough, I would think about doing a line. But I never fell back into it, and eventually it's gone away, but I can still remember so many of my high experiences and many great euphoric-feeling times on it. But pot never makes me feel like that. You know, in a weird way, my mother's cancer pulled me out of it. I had to be the one to step up and take care of her. I couldn't take care of her while I was high."

"Do you think if you hadn't been given a reason to stop, you would have stopped on your own?" I asked. "Or do you think you would have just self-destructed?"

"I was only a few steps from self-destructing. I lived on that ledge for a long time. If anyone I worked with actually had any sense or any experience with drugs, and if they hadn't thought I was some kind of Puritan, they would have known I was high. And I would have lost everything. It could have ended badly. It could have ended with felony convictions."

102

As he excavated the bones of his relationships, I looked for any resemblance to me. A sliver of who I am, of what I wasn't telling him. Assemble these slivers, and he would see the relationship he didn't know he had with me.

"Would you do anything differently?" I asked.

"No. I made it through life. I made it to where I am. I'm good. The exes who were dicks to me, I don't wish them any ill will. The guys I was a dick to, I feel badly for that. There are other ways to get out of a situation without treating someone the way someone else treated you. What is it, an eye for an eye leads to a blind world?"

"I've never heard that before," I said.

"I don't think about legitimate times when it wasn't working. I think about times when it was a crap excuse, or a selfish reason. Just because pain gets passed on, doesn't mean you have to do it intentionally."

"Maybe you just latch on to unavailable men."

"I try to get invested. I go into things with the intention of being in a relationship. I think I get hurt more because I invest emotion in relationships that don't have the possibility of really going where I want them to go. But however long the road, it leads to the right place."

"And you have found the booby prize."

"The which prize?"

"The booby prize."

"The booby?"

"The booby prize. I am the twenty-five-cent prize at the bottom of the box of Cracker Jacks. It's not really a prize. It's worth like a quarter. You've paid two dollars for the box, and the Cracker Jacks are stale, and the prize is something that doesn't even work or breaks after the first time or something."

"I love my prize," he said.

A few days shy of six months is the longest relationship Jay had had.

Until me. By only about three weeks.

And now I'm another ex-boyfriend, another story about an imploded relationship.

3

The night I decided to throw Jay a party for his 29th birthday, we got into a fight about how often he got high with Brett. We had been drinking, and he wanted me to stop giving him a hard time about using drugs, and I wanted him to stop using.

He told me if I brought it up again, then he wasn't sure he could be with me.

"I won't bring it up again," I said.

But a plan was already beginning to form.

If he wouldn't listen to me about how his drug use affected him, then he would surely listen to himself. And to do that, all I had to do was download a recording app to an iPhone I no longer used, turn it on, and hide it in his room on a night he planned to get high with Brett.

At the time, all of this seemed reasonable. He had made me promise to do whatever I needed to do to stop him from using.

Each time I tell this part of the story, none of it seems reasonable—until I say that I bought Jay a ring and asked him to marry me.

Recording him and his friends using drugs, without him knowing, sounds quite sane in comparison.

I asked him to marry me because I wanted to ask him, and because I thought that if he said yes then nothing his friends said or did would take him from me. I asked him because I felt desperate.

I ordered the ring from a metalworker I found online who took custom orders. I guessed at Jay's ring size. No real way of asking Jay his ring size without tipping him off that I was buying—or had bought—him a ring.

I brought the ring with me to his apartment for several days before I gave it to him. We were in his bed, just talking, and the moment felt right.

I took the ring out of its box, and I put it on Jay's left ring finger.

He looked at it, then at me, then started to cry. He held his hand up, then turned his hand upside down. The ring fell off.

"I'll get it re-sized," I said.

"I love it. I love you."

He unhooked the necklace he had on, and he put the ring on the chain.

"Will you marry me?"

The question needed to be asked; his answer needed to be given.

"Yes," he said.

That night, on my way home, I texted him: "I want to spend the next fifty-seven years with you. I want to wake up next to you, and go to bed next to you, and take care of you. I want to see the life our children will have. I want adventures, and I want to travel. There may come times when we want nothing more than to walk away, but I promise to always come back."

And he responded.

"You know you will have to tell me all of this in person. I will not settle for a text-message proposal. I won't even settle for a bedroom proposal while we are in bed. I want you there, on one knee, and I want to see you cry. I want it in public and messy. I don't want you to ask me safely. I want to know that you mean forever when you ask me for forever. And when I say yes, and I am definitely saying yes, then you will know that I mean forever and that no one else will do. I want to look into your eyes when you are proposing, and I want you to look into mine when I say yes."

"Does this mean we're not engaged?" I asked.

"I love you, and I want to marry you," he said. "We're engaged."

But can you consider a couple engaged if they don't tell anyone that they're engaged? Because we didn't tell anyone. I suggested we wait until after the party, so it didn't become a birthday-slash-engagement party. Jay agreed. He wanted us to tell Holly before we told anyone else.

The night before his birthday party, he, Brett, and another friend decided they were going to smoke until they had smoked as much of an ounce of weed as they could. That afternoon, I came over at lunch, since he was home from work, and while he was plating some sushi, I turned on the app and left the phone under his bed.

All night, I waited for him to text and let me know he had found the phone and that we were over. But I didn't hear from him, and at midnight, when I texted to see if he and his friends were still together, he didn't respond.

He's found the phone, I thought.

Just thinking that my relationship with him was over caused my heart to beat faster, and an area under the right side of my ribs to hurt.

At around three in the morning, I texted him again, and he responded that his friends were gone. I asked if he wanted me to come over. At his apartment, I took off my clothes, crawled under his comforter, and when he kissed me, I knew something was different.

"How high are you?" I asked.

"I don't feel very high at all."

But I knew better.

In the morning, while Jay was getting ready to go to work, I retrieved my phone from under Jay's bed. Its battery was nearly gone.

I got home as Holly was getting ready to leave for work.

"Couldn't sleep, so I went out for a while," I told her.

She didn't say anything.

She was in the bathroom getting ready, and I stood in the doorway. She looked into the mirror and saw me standing there. She raised one eyebrow, a question.

"Last night, I recorded Jay and his friends getting high."

Jay, whom she still only thinks is a good friend of mine.

"Why?" Holly asked.

"I need him to know who he is when he's high."

"That's not your job."

"But I think I'm the only person in his life who can help him."

"If you need to record him getting high to show him what his drug use is doing to him, and to you, then you maybe should reconsider his place in your life."

"I know," I said.

She knew how much time I spent with him, how often he used, and didn't like that I brought Avery into Jay's home.

"I don't understand why you need to hang out with him so much," she said.

"He's just a good friend," I said.

Holly left for work, and I took Avery to the Charles River for our regular Saturday walk. I put in my headphones and pressed play on the recording.

I did not feel like a voyeur, listening to what happened the night before. I did not feel like I was doing anything wrong.

Jay bought an ounce of weed from his roommate, sold half of it to Brett, and then the two of them packed a bowl and smoked it until it was gone. They were getting hungry, but before leaving for the grocery store, Brett asked if Jay would be his life coach.

"I'm just not sure what to do with my life, and I trust that you'll help me figure stuff out," Brett said.

"Of course, I can help," Jay said.

"We can smoke and just talk."

"OK."

"You know Will can't come over when we're doing this."

"I'll make sure he knows."

They left, and I forwarded through the recording until I could hear voices. Jay and Brett and a third friend, one I didn't know very well. The three of them smoking and talking about what to watch.

"I'm tired of fighting with him," he said. "I'm tired of dating someone who won't get high with me and who judges me when I do."

"It's about time you find someone better than Will," Brett said.

Jay asked for the bong. The weed in it was almost done.

"Want to do something else?" said by someone, maybe Brett, maybe Jay, but I couldn't distinguish the voice because I was crying, and Avery was asking for me, and the birds, the Goddamn birds on the side of the river, were loud and the sky itself seemed loud, or at the very least seemed like it was about to fall, or that it was already falling and I was the only one who knew it.

"I have these," Jay said.

I imagined that he pointed to those bottles of pills lined up on his bookshelf. I imagined him opening one of the bottles and dumping a few of the pills into his hand.

I could hear Jay crushing the pills. And I could hear him snorting the pills. And I could hear his friends snorting the pills. And I could hear him suggest that they do more.

I turned off the recording, took the headphones out of my ears, and I stopped walking.

"Daddy sad?" Avery asked.

"A little," I said.

"I love you Daddy," Avery said, and then he asked for some cheesy chips.

I called Holly and told her what I heard on the recording.

"I don't know what to do."

"You don't hang out with him. You don't take my son into his home. You figure out why you felt the need to record him using drugs."

"I shouldn't have recorded him," I said.

"You shouldn't have," she said.

Holly works at a hospital where men and women struggling with drug addictions, among other things, are sent. She talks with these people, and she tries to find them places where they can get help.

"You know what we say at work?" she asked. "How can you tell when an addict is lying?"

"I don't know."

"They open their mouths."

4

If only the key on its chain around my neck opened a wardrobe to another land or a gate into a secret garden. If it, like a divining rod, sensed rabbit holes to wonderland.

Heavy, this key on its chain around my neck.

I distracted myself with his birthday party preparations, but couldn't stop thinking about the sound of them snorting something.

I called Jay, who was at work.

"Did you guys do cocaine last night?" I asked.

Avery was playing in the living room and watching TV.

Maybe he'll tell me that he snorted pills, then his doing it won't be so bad.

"You know I don't put anything up my nose."

"But I'm in your room," I said. He wouldn't know that I wasn't in his room. "There is powder on your desk that looks like coke."

His computer desk was the only place where he could have crushed the pills.

"If you taste the powder, and your lips tingle, then you'll know that it's cocaine," Jay said. "It isn't cocaine."

Kind of ballsy, his telling me to taste the powder, not that he denied that there could be powder on his desk.

"What about pills?" I asked. "Did you guys snort pills?"

"No," Jay said.

He didn't hesitate.

"Maybe it's not powder," I said. "I'll just clean it up."

"Thanks, Rabbit," he said. "I'm excited for tonight."

"Me too," I said. "I'll see you after work."

"I love you," he said.

"Me too."

Two hours before Jay finished his shift, I went to his apartment and set up. Tied balloons to doorknobs and taped two to the outside of his front door; stretched butcher block paper along a wall in the hallway, so people could write Jay birthday messages; put vegetables and sushi on platters; put the cake in the refrigerator; and split two dozen red roses between three vases.

I wasn't sure I could get through the party without telling him what I knew. I considered leaving a note telling Jay that I wasn't feeling well. Then I thought that if I could pull off an affair for more than six months, I could pull off one birthday party.

I went home to get ready, and when I came back, I knew I'd be the first to arrive.

"This is all great, Rabbit," Jay said when I came inside his apartment. "Thank you for doing all of this."

"No problem," I said.

Jay kissed me.

"Hey, I know what that powder was that you found earlier," Jay said.

"What was it?" I asked.

"Sugar," Jay said.

"Sugar?"

"Sugar. I found some sugar in the bottom of the bag I take to work. A sugar packet must have broken inside it. I had my bag on the desk this morning, so some of the sugar must have fallen out."

He showed me the sugar crystals inside his bag.

"That must be it," I said.

I thought that he must have broken a sugar packet in his bag to cover up the pill powder he thought I found on his desk. Then I thought that maybe there had been sugar powder on his desk, and he had crushed the pills somewhere other than the desk. My lie revealing an actual truth. Sugar on his desk, since the pills were never there.

After a few other people arrived, we did shots, then switched to beer. I drank more than I had intended, but didn't feel drunk. Instead, I felt like I was committing the party to memory for later analysis. How Jay didn't hang out with me but instead hung out with Brett. How all of the couples who were there stood together, but Jay only stood with me once, and only when he asked if I was having a good time. How Jay disappeared into his bedroom with several people for several minutes.

I was alone at one point, sometime after midnight, and I was talking to myself, wondering why I was there, and how Jay would react if I left, and if I got what I deserved by recording a night when Jay did something more than pot.

Kathy told me that monologuing is a symptom of mania, and she suggested, when I told her about the party and the recording and the pills, that hearing the recording triggered a manic episode that likely didn't end until the nights I tried to kill myself.

While Jay was busy with some of his friends, I thought about leaving. I'd text Jay and let him know I was tired and wanted to get some sleep since I'd be alone with Avery the next day while Holly was at work. I wondered what the repercussions of my leaving would be.

I also thought that I could just as easily ask him to marry me. His friends would be there. It would be public. It could be messy. After, we could eat cake.

But I couldn't leave in the middle of the party, and I couldn't, in front of his friends, ask him to marry me.

St. Jude, the Trifecta of Saints

1

The Tobin Bridge spans more than two miles, connects Charlestown to Chelsea, and is the easiest and fastest way to drive into Boston from where Holly and I live. Dozens of people have jumped off of the bridge since it opened in 1950, including Charles Stuart, the prime suspect in his pregnant wife's murder. Dozens of others have been convinced not to jump.

I've avoided the bridge since the night—second night, really—I tried to kill myself. But a four-car accident has snarled traffic on the road I take into Boston to get to St. Elizabeth's, and I'm running late enough that I have no choice but to drive into Boston via the bridge. Bumper-to-bumper this morning on the bridge, and for every few feet I move forward, I'm stuck not moving for at least a minute, long enough to recognize the part of the bridge on which I had been standing, close to the edge.

I had recorded a suicide video before leaving for the bridge. Holly and Avery had been playing ball in the hallway outside our front door.

That night, I waited for Holly and Avery to fall asleep, and I snuck out. Walking to the elevator seemed to take longer than usual. Outside, I looked at the sky, and I looked at the stars, and I thought that Jay was under these same stars, probably with someone, probably high, probably on his way to being consoled and happy. His moving on guaranteed. Less than forty-eight hours after the end of our relationship.

When I reached the highest part of the Tobin Bridge that night, I stopped, turned off the car, undid my seatbelt, opened my door, and got out of the car. I looked at the four or five feet I'd have to walk to reach the edge of the bridge, and I thought about taking the first step, when I saw three cars approaching. I got back into my car.

No one stopped to find out why I was standing on the bridge.

I drove a few feet further, and got out of the car again. This time, I left on the hazard lights.

On the passenger seat, I left the necklace with the key to Jay's childhood bedroom, my phone, and a note asking Holly to watch the video on it.

Nothing made sense. Everything was ruined. Holly hated me. Jay hated me. I hated me. In time, Avery would hate me. Gravity held me to the bridge. I was trying to fight gravity. I no longer wanted to fight gravity. If this was love, then love was like falling, and my heart was gone, and I was gone, and everything was broken, and I was broken, and I was going out altogether like a candle. Have you seen what the flame of a candle looks like after the candle has been blown out? I wondered what would be left, once I was gone.

I was depressed. I had lost what I thought defined me. The mania that Kathy thinks began the day of the party had become depression. If in the hospital I felt like the color gray, that night on the bridge I felt translucent.

Just jump. It will all be over. You will jump, and you will fall, and if you get lucky you will be dead before you hit the water, and if you are still alive, you won't be for long since you will drown. Four minutes. I read somewhere that you can last four minutes without oxygen. I wouldn't wait four minutes. I'd fall into the water, and the water would be cold, and I'd open my mouth and drink until I felt like I had swallowed the entire river, and then I would be gone, the hazards on my car blinking, the note on the passenger seat waiting to be read.

The bridge under my feet swaying.

I took one step, then a second. I'd jump and I'd close my eyes and I'd hit the water and then everything would mostly be over. I wish something noble kept me from taking a third step, something related to Avery or to owing Holly more than another mess to clean up, but I didn't take a third step because I didn't think I would die. I thought I would jump, someone would rescue me, and I'd end up paralyzed or worse, unable to take care of myself, maybe confined to a hospital bed.

There's no one who will take care of me.

That's why I didn't take a third step, why I got back into my car, and why I drove over the bridge and into Boston, past a playground where Jay and I often took Avery.

My thoughts were faster than how long I needed to think my thoughts, and the cars I had seen on the bridge were there and then they weren't, and maybe I had invented the cars, and the headlights, and how much I wanted to die.

I called Holly.

"I need help," I said, when Holly answered the phone.

116

"You're not here. Where are you?"

"I'm at the Tobin Bridge. I was going to jump."

"Come home. We can get you help. Come home."

"OK."

"Do you need me to stay on the line with you until you get here?"

"No."

"Just come home," she said. "Everything will be OK."

2

Chris, the guy with anxiety, completes his two weeks on my fourth day of group therapy. Two or three more people are joining me and Erin on Wednesday.

"You'll be the senior member, so to speak."

"I feel like I'm still figuring out what I'm supposed to get out of this group."

"You may not even realize what you got out of the group until months from now," she says. "You'll face a situation, and you'll react or respond to it without thinking, and you'll realize that you've reacted or responded in a way that puts your best interests first. You'll know what to do. Don't ignore the voice in your head. Listen and follow through. Protect yourself and you will find other people around you willing to protect you, too."

Holly is cooking when I get home. Some kind of pasta and chicken dish. Avery is playing with his cars. Holly looks at me.

"What?" she asks. Pregnant enough to know that we are having a girl, who we months ago named Aurora. I've missed most of the prenatal appointments, though I'd gone with Holly to each appointment when she was pregnant with Avery. Unspoken, our decision that I'd not go with her to these appointments for and about Aurora. Even before Holly knew about Jay.

"Are you making enough for me to eat, too?" I ask.

"No," she says. "I don't have to cook for you anymore."

"I'll just make something when you're done cooking."

She adds more pasta to the pot.

"You can have some," she says.

I take off my shoes, untuck my shirt, and get on my hands and knees in the living room with Avery. He wraps his arms around my neck and pulls me to the ground.

"I love you, Daddy," he says.

"I love you, too," I say.

Avery rolls a car up my arm, across my back, and down my other arm. Then he does the same with a second, and then with a third car. I laugh, and Avery laughs, and I roll onto my side and tickle Avery under his arms, and the sound Avery makes when he is being tickled under his arms is one of the best sounds in the world, equal parts happy and funny and tickled and loved.

Holly watches me play with Avery. I turn in her direction, still on my side, and I toss Avery's cars back to him, so he can roll them across my body again. She turns back to the stove and lowers the heat.

3

Inside the Basilica of Our Lady of Perpetual Help, which is located in the Mission District of Boston, supplicants kneel in front of a picture of Our Mother of Perpetual Help. The picture is framed in gold, and rays, also made of gold, extend from the frame in all directions.

These rays are meant to symbolize all of the different ways Our Mother had extended into everyday life. On each side of the shrine to Our Mother, you will find two vases filled with crutches and canes. Our Mother, known for curing invalids and healing the sick.

In the painting, the Virgin Mary is holding her son, and the two are flanked by the Archangels Michael and Gabriel. While Mary cannot remove her son's burden, or ease the suffering he will endure, she and her embrace offer refuge.

I didn't know the story of Our Mother, the first time I went into Our Lady of Perpetual Help. All I knew about the church was that you can see the church's spires no matter where in the Mission District you are, if you know where to look. I went in to pray, despite my mostly agnostic view on religion. If I had told Jay what I did, he would have laughed. His Buddhist beliefs, while broad and encompassing, did not include tolerance for what he called charlatan attempts to scare you into good behavior.

I went in, and I lit a candle, and I asked for guidance. I wasn't comfortable asking Our Mother for help; I didn't think she'd give it. Instead, I prayed to St. Jude, Patron Saint of Hope, who is also the Patron Saint of Lost Causes and the Patron Saint of Desperate Cases.

When I picked St. Jude, I didn't know that I had picked the trifecta of saints.

After Jay told me about his mother, I started praying for her. And then I started praying for Holly to carry the baby to term.

On the afternoon of the last day that Jay and I were together, though I didn't know it was the afternoon of the last day that Jay and I would be together, I returned to Our Lady of Perpetual Help. Inside, six people were in front of the shrine. Their emergencies more important than mine, I thought. I stayed long enough to thank St. Jude for his help, but acknowledged that I created this mess and needed more than his intervention to clean it up.

I had hidden my phone in Jay's bedroom again that afternoon. Couldn't hide it under his bed, because the phone didn't have much of a charge. Hid it behind a bookcase, where I could also plug in the phone. Jay and Brett were planning to smoke the rest of what they had bought the night before the party. Brett also wanted to buy more weed, which Jay agreed to sell.

Jay's birthday was the next day. I had expected to be with him at midnight, but Brett's plans ruined mine.

I left the church, and was walking in the direction of downtown Boston, when I got a text from Jay, a video of him in the shower, playing with his penis.

I didn't respond to the text message until one minute past midnight. "Happy birthday," I wrote.

"Thank you, Rabbit," he responded.

When an invitation to come over didn't come, I fell asleep.

I woke up at three. I texted Jay, but he didn't respond. He sleeps with his phone next to his bed. He always hears when a text message comes in. I texted again. No response.

Maybe the phone is off, I thought. I called, and the phone rang enough times before going to voicemail so I knew the phone was on.

He's ignoring me, I thought.

He's found the phone, I thought.

What do I do now? I thought.

I got dressed and drove to his apartment. I unlocked the front door, walked up the stairs, and tried to unlock the door to his apartment. My key didn't turn.

He had changed the lock on his front door.

I called Jay, but this time the call went straight to voicemail.

He had turned off his phone, or he had pressed the ignore call button on his phone.

I thought about knocking, but I knew if I knocked, and if Jay's roommates came to the door, they would be happy to tell me that Jay no longer wanted me there.

I went home. I made and drank a pot of coffee. I made and drank a second pot of coffee. I filled out the birthday cards I had bought Jay. I made and drank a third pot of coffee.

On my way to work, I stopped at Jay's apartment. My key still didn't turn in the lock to his front door. I called. I knocked. I slid the cards under the door to his apartment.

I went to where he worked, walked into the employee's-only area, and asked where Jay was. He was working on his birthday so we could have an extra day off together the next week.

"He called in sick," one of his colleagues told me. She looked at me as if she knew something about me that I didn't know.

"He didn't tell me," I said.

I left the store, and then called Jay. Voicemail, another message, my fifth I think, since the night before.

"If you were going to call in, you should have let me know. I would have called in, too, and we could have spent your entire birthday together."

I was at work when he responded to my texts and phone calls:

"I found the phone. We are over. It is creepy. Don't call me. Don't text me. We're done. We're over. We're through."

The text-message break-up we had promised not to have. I called again and the call went straight to voicemail.

"Just talk to me. You need to understand why I did it."

He texted: "We are over. Do not call me. Do not text me. Do not contact me. We are over."

I was sitting in an empty office, and I was crying, and on Jay's twenty-ninth birthday, I became another ex-boyfriend.

I was no longer in control.

I was no longer balancing two relationships.

I was out of balance, falling up and falling down and wondering how I let everything get to this point and wondering how long Jay would need before he forgave me and told me he loved me.

I called Holly, who was at work.

"I left the phone in his room again last night, and he found out," I said. "He doesn't want to be my friend anymore."

"He's your best friend," she said. "He'll get over it. Tell him that you're worried about him, and that we don't want him around Avery."

"He won't come around," I said. "He makes decisions and sticks to them."

"He'll come around. He clearly cares about you and Avery."

"I'm going to go home," I said. "Can you meet me there?"

"Can we talk about this after work?"

"No. My heart is breaking," I said. And then, "We've been dating. I love him."

"I'm coming home," Holly said.

Then she hung up.

She and I got to our home around the same time. She was carrying a bag from Dunkin Donuts, and a coffee. We rode the elevator to the third floor together, but didn't talk. Inside our home, Holly put her bag and coffee on a counter in the kitchen. Then I told her everything I could think to tell her. She wouldn't cry in front of me. When she had to cry, she left the living room and closed and locked the bathroom door behind her, even though we had long ago stopped closing and locking bathroom doors.

4

During my last day of the partial-hospital program, Erin gives me the name and phone number of a therapist.

"I talked to her. She thinks she can help you. I think you've done some great work, but I'm concerned you might relapse if you don't find someone outside to talk with."

"He's not talking to me," I say. "How can I relapse?"

"He's not talking to you now. He may talk to you again in the future."

God, I hope so, I think. Please let me be that ex whom he can't forget.

"I don't think that's going to happen, but I'll call her," I say. "I'll set up an appointment."

"I really think you're going to get through this, and I think that everything is going to be OK, and I think, in time, you will understand why all of this had to happen the way it has happened."

"I feel like such a lost cause," I say. Doesn't matter how many candles I'd light. Even divine intervention couldn't engineer a comeback.

"You need to remember that everything changes. People change. Relationships change."

"I changed."

"You changed. And you will keep changing."

"How do I know if I'm changing for the better?"

"I think you'll know, Will," she says.

"I wanted so badly for it to work with him," I say.

"I know," she says. "You'll find someone else, and that someone else will be different and it will still be wonderful and you will not compete with his addictions, because I think you will not let yourself get into a situation where you have to compete with his addictions."

"I had this picture in my head of what life with him and the kids and Holly would be like. I thought I could have it all. I thought I finally could be whole and happy."

"In order to be whole and happy, you need people in your life who are whole and happy," she says.

Another slogan in a place built on slogans.

"He isn't whole and happy. Give it time. Give yourself some room to breathe. Give yourself some room to live. Don't rush into anything because you think you need to be with someone. Be with yourself; the rest will come into focus when it comes."

5

Holly needed time to herself after I told her about Jay, so I agreed to pick Avery up from day care while she went out with a friend. On my way to get Avery, I stopped at a local drugstore and bought two bottles of sleeping pills.

So I was already feeling desperate, when the police officer knocked on my door.

"Are you William Henderson?" the officer asked.

"Yes."

He asked me if I knew Jay. Of course the police officer said Jay's full name. First and last. Not his middle, which even I, more than six months after learning it, couldn't pronounce.

"He has filed a restraining order against you. You are barred from contacting him, going to his home, or going to his place of employment. Do you understand?"

"Yes."

I had to sign a paper. I didn't look at what I was signing.

"Consider this service of notice."

"Thank you."

I called Holly. "He took out a restraining order against me."

"What the fuck?" Holly actually sounded angry on my behalf. "He's labile, Will. There's no reason he needs a restraining order."

"I know."

"How's Avery?" she asked.

Avery was playing with his cars in the bedroom, using different voices for the cars. I loved hearing him give his cars personalities and voices.

"He's fine."

"I'll be home later," she said.

"I'll be here."

I swallowed a cocktail of Motrin PM, Melatonin, and white wine. I was on autopilot. I had passed how I felt and moved into not wanting to feel. I locked the front door, so

Avery couldn't let himself out and run into the hallway. I watched him play.

I put some food on a plate, and filled three cups with juice. I left the food and juice where Avery could reach.

I went to the couch, and I started to disappear. Or to feel what disappearing must feel like. I couldn't feel my hands. I couldn't feel my feet. I couldn't feel my head. My heart, shattered, I could feel. Slowly, still familiar, this beating. At night, in bed, Jay with his head on my chest, listening to my heartbeat, telling me how loud my heart sounded, when his head was on my chest, in bed, at night.

On a different day, Holly had to tell me that when she got home, she woke me up, asked what I had taken, and suggested we go to the hospital.

I kept telling her I would be fine if she would just let me sleep.

All the King's Horses, All the King's Men

1

I can hear the noise of the bar behind me. People outside laughing and smoking, unable to bring out their drinks without violating one or more of Boston's arcane liquor laws. It is warm and I am sweating in my shirt, something I couldn't fit into two months ago, and likely still can't fit into but wore tonight anyway. My friends, Murdock and Sandro, say they want to hang out, but I know they really want to check and see how I'm doing.

I agreed to meet them for a drink tonight because I was tired of being at home with Holly and Avery. Not tired of them, just tired of being at home with them, listening to Avery challenge Holly and to her when she yells at him. Last night, Holly and I watched a movie after Avery went to bed. It was a love story.

I'm drunk, and I think I only had one and maybe half of another drink. Almost a month since I used white wine to wash down the pills and nothing with alcohol in it to drink since.

I drank a clear white chocolate martini—the drink I always order when I go to this specific bar in the South End. The bar is one of a couple that mostly serves a gay clientele. Jay and I went there once. We didn't stay long. We left after he pointed out a guy in the bar that he thought was cute.

No one at St. Elizabeth's believed me when I said that all I needed was Jay to let me explain—really explain—my actions.

But his decision to let me do just that is all getting back together with him took.

That and ice cream and letting him have time with Avery.

I'm rushing this telling. The alcohol is making me rush this telling. I'm walking toward my car. I told Murdock and Sandro I was tired. They suggested we hang out again next weekend.

Every few seconds I look at my phone for a text message response to a text I probably shouldn't have sent but did anyway. I'll blame the alcohol, when he responds. I'll tell him that I've been drinking and he knows never to take me seriously when I've been drinking and I'll ask him where he wants to have dinner tomorrow. That was his request—dinner together to work out reunification details, like we need to broker the removal of a wall dividing East from West.

I'm walking over an overpass, but I'm not going to jump. This is a new and improved Will.

Will 2.0—that's what I told Jay to think of me as.

2

A week ago, I asked Holly again if she would consider getting in touch with Jay and figure out a time to trade back our stuff. He had so much of my stuff, and I had so little of his, that it felt unfair, his keeping the things he had, which included several parts of a sterling silver set of service that Holly and I received as a wedding gift. I didn't need Holly to tell me that she wanted the set in our divorce to know that she wanted the set in our divorce.

"He is not keeping our dishes," she told me. "If there isn't another way, then I'll get in touch with him."

"I guess I could call the police and see if they would help me. Maybe they could go with me, or get in touch with him on my behalf."

"Maybe," Holly said, though she didn't sound hopeful.

Six days ago, I called the police department in the town where Jay lives. I sat in the same office where I was when he text-messaged me our break up, and I explained to the police officer who answered that my ex-boyfriend had several things that belonged to me and my wife and son and I wasn't sure how to get them back with the restraining order in place.

This officer looked up the restraining order in his system, but couldn't find it.

"According to our records, there is no restraining order in place against you," this officer told me.

He told me his name, but I can't remember it.

The police could intervene, he said, but only if I filed a stolen property report.

"Even if he bought some of the things he has for me and my son?"

"Even if," the officer said. "If you file a stolen property report, then we'd send someone out to his house, and if we found the items you had reported stolen, we'd arrest him."

"Arrest him arrest him?" I asked.

"Yes," he said. "We'd collect the things we find from the list of items you report as stolen, and we'd bring them and him back to the station for processing."

If he is arrested, he'd be fired for sure, I thought. His boss is likely looking for any reason to let him go. And if I have him arrested, then I lose any chance I have of winning him back.

"I'll let you know," I said. "Thank you for the information."

I explained to Holly what seemed like my only option, and it wasn't much of an option at that. She agreed that having Jay arrested was unnecessary.

"I'll text him and see when a good time is to switch back your stuff."

He told her that he would have everything ready that afternoon. If she didn't want to see him, he could leave everything on the front porch of his house and she could leave for him what I had of his.

"I don't want to see him," Holly said. "I'll go after I pick up Avery from school."

While she handled getting everything back from Jay, I went with a friend to a yoga class. I had promised Erin I would join a gym and take a yoga class.

But Holly hadn't traded back with Jay by the time I got out of class. I agreed to stay later at the gym. I found a free treadmill and I started walking.

"All I need to give him is what was in the plastic bag?" Holly asked.

"Yes," I replied.

And later: "He can't find everything. He says he's missing one glove and some tools."

"I want the gloves," I said. "He needs to find the missing glove."

Though if he couldn't find it, I thought, then he and I would forever be part of a matched set.

"OK," she texted a couple of minutes later. "He found it, but he still can't find some tools you loaned him. He's going to give you some money for them. And he erased your phone, but he's going to write out instructions for how you can restore it to its factory settings."

Of course he erased my phone, since it was how I recorded him and his friend getting high. I'm surprised he didn't break it.

"Can you tell him that I'm sorry? Tell him I regret everything that happened."

"OK," she said, even though I doubt she wanted to say any of those things to him.

"And don't let him see Avery," I texted to her. "I don't want them to see each other."

"I'm not going to take him out of the car," Holly said. "He's going to leave everything on his porch. I don't think I'm going to see him at all."

And she didn't. She got there, and everything was arranged in a large box she couldn't carry on her own. She had to get a couple of men who live across the street from Jay to lift the box into her car.

Those same men were always out on their porch, and when I'd leave at two and three in the morning, usually after sex, I saw those men and I wondered if they knew what I had been doing just five or 10 minutes earlier.

"You'll have to get the box out of my car," she texted to me, and she told me she was on her way home.

I got off the treadmill and wiped it down with a towel.

"I'll come home now, too," I told her.

"He sent me something to share with you if you want it," she said.

"Send it to me."

She forwarded me a text from him to her to give to me: *I still love Will. I just can't overcome the other stuff. I wish all of you wonder.*

I knew he still loved me.

When I got home, I read and re-read his text message, and I decided that responding couldn't hurt.

"Goodbye, Horse," I texted, and he replied in less than one minute.

"Goodbye, Rabbit."

He and I, overly dramatic, with our goodbyes and I'll always love you and midnight car rides to psychiatric hospitals. But everything has always felt heightened with him, kind of how a car accident feels.

Holly and I were in a car accident when we moved from Seattle to Boston. We could have died, we later learned, but what saved us was my decision the day before we were scheduled to leave to trade in my small car for an SUV. Had we been in the small car and had the same accident, she and I likely would have died on a mostly deserted road near Paradise, Montana.

I was driving, and while we had promised her parents that we would stop for the night before driving from Idaho into Montana, I kept going. We were about an hour into Montana when I drove across black ice, lost control of the SUV, careened across the other lane on our side of the road and crashed into the railing along the median. The collision caused our airbags to eject. I remember watching Holly's face and her airbag connect, but then I was face down in my airbag. She and I felt the car bounce off the railing and slide back across the mountain road and crash into the railing on the other side of the road.

You feel like everything happens in slow motion when you're in an accident, like you see it happen right before it does. You know you should try to stop it, but you can't. Almost like you fall a bit out of sync with time, like you're living three or four seconds slower than everyone else. The accident has happened, and you just need to catch up with it.

She and I driving from Seattle to Boston, transporting the things too fragile to ship via freight with the rest of our stuff, like our four cats and pet bird. And the hood of the SUV crumpled back against the windshield and did you know that airbags deflate once the vehicle is no longer in motion. I was pressed back against my seat and then I wasn't, and I asked Holly if she was OK and she asked if I was OK and we didn't have cell reception for a while but then we did and though the car, and half of the things inside of it, was totaled, she and I and our pets were fine.

You catch up with the accident and it's a flurry of phone calls and arrangements and figuring out how to ship everything in boxes provided by sympathetic staff at a motel with 23 rooms to rent.

The accident happened seven years and three days before Jay and I met. My collision with him almost derailed by an actual collision.

He and I had crashed, but we hadn't died.

You can always buy a new car. You can always rebuild bridges, even when they've been mostly burned.

I went upstairs, and Holly was making dinner and Avery was playing with his toys. Holly had brought up one bag of my stuff.

"There's more in my car," she said.

"I'll get it later," I said. "I can't look at any of it now."

I sat on the couch, took off my shoes, and took my phone out of my pocket.

Goodbye, Rabbit.

I couldn't let goodbye be goodbye.

3

"Holly shared your last text. I still love you, too, even after everything," I wrote him in response.

"I'm still terribly hurt," he responded. "I think we can eventually be friends, despite my rules. I cannot be with you as my partner, but I can see a friendship again eventually. But you had no right bringing me into your marriage and lying to me about it."

"I wanted to tell you, but you said you'd been hurt by a married man before."

"And now I've been hurt by another married man," he said. "So many times I knew there was something more that you weren't telling me."

"You know everything now," I said. "If we can be friends again one day, then that will be a good day."

"I can't see you yet. And I'm not sure when I can," he said. "You can e-mail, and I'll respond to text messages here and there."

"OK."

"I don't know how you held it together as well as you did, living so closely with the both of us."

I wasn't holding it together very well, I wanted to say, but before I could say anything, he sent another text.

"Does Holly know I didn't know?"

"I told her everything an hour or so after you broke up with me," I said. "I couldn't lie to her anymore."

"Now is when I needed to meet you. You were a great partner, and I'm sure you're one thousand times better now. I'm sure you feel free and new. I wish I had just reinvented, rediscovered or accepted myself."

"Your ex-boyfriend doesn't live here anymore," I said. "You'll see. I'm Will 2.0."

"Well, this is who and where we are right now. We need to work toward a friendship. I'd like to meet Will someday. That is how I have to think about it right now."

"I understand."

"I wanted to call you when Holly sent me the e-mail. I was scared. I also worried that if I called and it wasn't to take you back, that you might try harder to end it."

"I didn't want to die. I just didn't know how to ask for help," I said. "Don't blame yourself. I don't."

"I don't blame myself," he said. "I just wanted to help you."

"I needed to go through it alone," I said. "And I had Holly and Avery."

A couple of minutes passed, and I thought maybe he had heard enough or had fallen asleep. It wouldn't have been the first time he had fallen asleep while we were texting. But then my phone vibrated with another message from him.

"By the way, the pills were just that once. I don't want you to have to worry and think that I snort stuff all the time. But I'm sure the audio told you that already if you listened. What *is* in the audio?"

"You snorting pills and getting high and making fun of me and ignoring my text at 2 a.m."

"That's it?"

"I couldn't listen to any more of it."

Except I had. I lied to him. I couldn't tell him that that night he confessed to his friends that there was someone he wanted to get to know better, mostly because the guy looked like he was a stoner. Had I told Jay that that was part of the recording, I thought I would scare him away. Frightened animals don't just bite the nearest hand; they also run away.

"I don't remember making fun of you. I'm sorry, but I was high most likely," he said. "Not that it's OK either way."

A few minutes passed before he texted again.

"My head is full, Rabbit. I need to go to bed. I'll want more answered, just not tonight."

Holly didn't ask me who I had been texting, and I didn't offer an explanation. But I stayed up later than usual, in case he texted again wanting to know something else.

4

I hand-to-God planned to respect his not feeling ready to see me yet. If he and I were going to get back together— and I knew we would—then I had to let him set the parameters, and I had to show him how well I could toe his lines.

Except the next day he asked me about our bench, the one near his store on which he had written "I wish you wonder." He wanted to know if I had scribbled out the message. And I told him I hadn't.

He believed me, or seemed to. Maybe he wanted to believe me, though he knows better than most how easily I can lie to those I love. Because of course I had gone back to that bench and scribbled out the message. Even if you knew what he had written there, you wouldn't be able to pick out any of the letters

I did it a couple of weeks ago, on my way to one of the partial-hospital sessions. I told myself I did it to erase a reminder of my relationship with him, but I did it to hurt him. I thought he'd see the message had been scribbled out and would know I had done it. Who else would have? The bench isn't exactly in the most public of places.

I told him I didn't scribble out the message on the bench, and I started feeling guilty for lying to him as well as for doing it. To make amends, I hatched a plan to replace the message with a new one on a different bench, a message more fitting for the current state of our relationship.

So on Wednesday, two days after he and I resumed contact, I went to the park near his store during my lunch break. I picked a bench far from the one he had marked, and I wrote on it a lyric from a song to which I had introduced him. I wouldn't need to tell him what I had done. He would see the bench when he saw the bench.

I was about to leave, and when I turned in the direction where I had parked my car, I saw him walking toward me.

Which meant that he had seen me here and decided to approach.

That should be important right? That he saw me first and still came over to say hi? I want to remember everything just how it happened, because one day these tiny details will be important.

He said hi and I said hi and he asked me how I was and I told him I was fine and I asked him how he was and he told me he was fine and then we stood there, staring.

"I wasn't expecting to see you," I said.

"I'm on break."

"Didn't you get your break hours ago?"

I know his schedule as well as I know mine.

"It's been busy today."

He smiled at me, looked down and started to laugh. I looked down as well to see what was funny.

We were wearing matching shoes, gray with white piping and gray laces. We each bought a pair a few weeks before we broke up. The store had had a buy one get one half-off sale.

"I have to go," I said, even though going was the last thing I wanted to do.

He hugged me then, and I collapsed a little into him before he let go and I let go and we stood there, still within hugging distance.

"Talk later?" I asked, and he agreed.

I didn't really have to rush back to work, but I was afraid of saying or doing something to scare him off.

"I'm sorry," I texted him, when I was back at work. "I know you didn't want to see me."

"True. I didn't want to see you yet, but it wasn't that bad," he replied. "The park kind of feels like neutral territory. How are you?"

"I think the universe has a sick sense of humor, bringing us together the way it did. But I'm OK. You?"

"I'm crying a bit, but I'm OK."

"I'm sorry."

"I could have turned around and walked back. The universe figured we were meant to talk. Just like sometimes I'm supposed to get in the car, even when I don't think I want to."

"I wanted to kiss you," I confessed.

"I told you I want to be friends," he said. "It will take time. I still love you, and I always will."

"Giving up seems like a waste."

"It's a lot," he said. "I worry that I won't trust you like I need to be able to."

"I'll re-earn your trust."

I meant it at the time, and I still mean it. I want him to know that I won't lie to him about anything more significant than holiday gifts and surprise vacations.

He never promised to re-earn my trust.

I don't think he thinks he's done anything to break it.

That same evening, I convinced him to meet for coffee after my yoga class. Between seeing me in the park and our coffee date, he shaved his head.

I figured he did it because he knows how much I liked him with a shaved head.

We talked for an hour about nothing really. His job and his mother and Avery and how Holly and I plan to divide our possessions into his and hers. He told me about his plans to buy a Wii; I told him that Holly is keeping our Wii.

"I want to figure out a way to have you in my life," he said. "I need to have you and Avery in my life. I'm not sure what that means, but I don't want to lose you."

"You can't lose a person," I said. "Avery and I are always here."

Echoes of what the social worker told me.

Some day you're going to be in a situation, and you're going to respond in a way that will show you just how much you're learning here, Erin had said.

"I'm not even supposed to be here, and neither are you."

"What do you mean?"

"The restraining order."

That.

"Didn't it expire after a week?" I asked.

"No. I showed up for the hearing, and you didn't. It was granted and is in effect for a year. I'll have to tell you about that day some time."

How about you tell me how you're going to drop it?, I thought. Let's talk about that instead.

But Jay didn't tell me that he's going to drop the restraining order, and I didn't ask him to. With the restraining order, he has power over me, and not feeling powerless is what all of his rules protect against.

"Holly and I are having a daughter," I told him, even though I knew he knew. "We're going to call her Aurora."

"You had mentioned that name as a possibility."

He didn't tell me that Holly had told him. I loved him a little more because he kept secret that Holly had told him, thinking that she hadn't told me that she had told him.

After we finished our coffee, he said he had to go. I had wanted to spend more time with him. Not at his apartment, but at another neutral place. Even back at the park. There is a trail that, if you follow it, leads to a pond. I wanted to go there, watch the sun set, and then kiss him.

A kiss by a pond is what this story needed.

But he didn't bring up hanging out together any longer.

140

"Maybe we could make a habit of meeting for coffee after yoga on Wednesdays?" I asked.

"I'd like that," Jay said. "But in time. I need space, and I want to be able to talk about things and see how us as friends works. I need you to be prepared for the fact that I may only want friendship with you in the end. I can't say right now, and I'm not comfortable pushing myself to make a black-and-white decision about the future and what it holds or doesn't hold. I think we need to work on being friends. I need to feel like I can let you back into my house. I don't feel like that right now."

"We've taken on water," I said. "But we haven't sunk."

"I know we haven't sunk. If we'd sunk then we wouldn't be talking. But a few days of texting and coffee is only the start. You will have to earn my trust again, and that's not going to be easy, and I'm not going to lie and say it would be."

6

I rented an apartment, the first place in more than 10 years where I'll live alone. I texted Jay after I found the apartment, just to let him know that that's what I had done. He offered to help me move.

"But you don't trust me in your apartment," I said to him.

"I don't know that I don't," he said.

The night I met Jay, I drove past the apartment that is now my home.

"I'd love your help," I said.

If he helped me arrange things, then when he started spending the night and eventually moved in he'd feel as at home in it as I would.

"Hey, I've been meaning to tell you that that last video I sent you of me in the shower wasn't a fuck-you video. I was just being silly," he said.

I had called the video a fuck-you video in those letters I wrote him during my inpatient stay at St. Elizabeth's.

"I didn't take it as a fuck-you video at the time," I said. "Only after."

"It wasn't meant like that at any point," he said. "Nothing I did was ever meant to hurt you. Everything I did was to protect myself."

"You're still protecting yourself," I said.

"I operate as logically as I can. It's my nature. Love doesn't understand logic. They are not friends. I am still protecting myself. You promised to protect me and you unintentionally hurt me. I am doing the best I can to accommodate love and logic."

Love and logic are strange bedfellows, but Jay explaining his distance this way is who he is.

And I love him, illogical as loving him is.

"We can just be friends," I said. "Just knowing you're doing well is enough."

"That's all I can offer right now," he said. "I know that we have the essence of us still, and that that may never go away, even as friends. We're both making a lot of changes right now, and our friendship is the part of our relationship we need right now. We're still us, Will. No words or titles or Facebook statuses change that. Stand next to me and tell me how you feel. There's no loss of connection there. But that doesn't mean that rushing back in is the right thing. If we can be friends and eventually

142

best friends, then I think that that is where the payoff is. It may be a slow process, but when we get there, it will be as seamless as it has always been."

"Does it make sense to say I've felt halved since we broke up?"

"I've felt the same way. My immediate instinct is to be with you again, but a solid friendship over time is the way we do that."

I didn't tell him that I don't believe in small breaks. A break is a break; small ones widen over time. So I agreed with him, even though I knew that time could not fix what was broken. Two halves do not make a whole when it comes to a healthy relationship.

"Do you want to meet for ice cream tonight?" I asked.

"Where?"

"Well, Holly is going out later, so I was going to take Avery to the Charles River and go for a walk, but we could meet you instead."

"I'll wait for you," he said.

I didn't need him to tell me that he'd wait for me outside of Park Street Station and bring food to feed the pigeons. I just knew that he'd wait for me outside of Park Street Station and bring food to feed the pigeons.

And he was there, surrounded by pigeons.

Avery, who hadn't seen Jay in nearly one month, called out Jay's name as we walked up to him.

"I missed you, buddy," Jay said, and he hugged Avery. Avery held onto Jay's neck, and Jay looked at me. His eyes were wet. And he was smiling. And I thought he would kiss me back, if I kissed him.

"Want some ice cream?" he asked Avery.

"Yes," Avery said.

We walked in the direction of Newbury Street, toward an ice cream shop about halfway down the street. The last time I was on Newbury Street was the night before Jay's birthday, when he and I were still together, and I received the video that wasn't a fuck-you video of him in the shower.

Jay bought our ice cream, and then he and I took turns feeding Avery.

"Ani DiFranco is coming," Jay said. "Brett and I are going."

"That will be fun," I said. I waited for him to invite me, but he didn't. "I might get a ticket. I wouldn't stand with you or anything."

"You should, Rabbit," he said. "It will be a good show."

We finished our ice cream, and we walked back in the direction of Boston Common so Jay could catch a train to his apartment and Avery and I could walk back to my car. We stopped across the street from where Jay needed to get on the train. A police officer was standing against a building. Jay hugged Avery, and then looked at me. He reached for me, and I reached for him, and we hugged a few seconds longer than friends hug.

"Thank you for all of this," Jay said.

"You're welcome," I said.

I watched him walk away, and then I pushed Avery's stroller in the direction of my car. At a red light, Avery asked for juice, and when I got Avery's juice, I realized I still had a bag in which Jay had put his leftover ice cream.

I called Jay to tell him I had his ice cream, and he told me that he had taken out his ice cream but left the bag.

And then we said nothing for a few seconds.

"Thank you again for coming out, and for bringing Avery," Jay said. "I love you."

"I love you, too."

Through the phone I could hear the sound of the approaching train, and I knew Jay would have to go. I thought he was waiting for me to say something, and I was waiting for him to say something, and neither of us said anything until I said, "I'll talk to you in the morning."

"Until tomorrow," he said, and he hung up.

What I should have said is come back. Don't get on the train. I'm turning around. I'll meet you back at the corner. Let's do something else. Let's walk around until Avery falls asleep.

And I think Jay would have come back, because he would have wanted to come back, and we would have met at the corner where we went our separate ways, and I would have put the brake on Avery's stroller, and I would have stepped into him and he would have hugged me and I would have wrapped my hands around the back of his neck and we would have kissed for the first time in more than three weeks. That police officer who had been standing against the building would have needed to look away, because that's what people do when they see two people so madly in love.

And then last night, the night after Jay and I had ice cream, he went out with friends and I stayed in with Holly and Avery and we watched a movie. I woke up at 3 in the morning, and checked my phone, expecting a text from Jay letting me know he had arrived home OK.

"Is everything all right?" I texted him. I knew my text would wake him up if he was asleep.

Not once did I think that he was on a date.

"I love you, and I'm OK," he replied. "I know you're it. My it. Us. You, me, Holly, Avery, and Aurora. We can and will get there."

"Really?" I responded.

"Yes," he said. "I'm yours. You're mine. I love you."

"That was the first time you typed Aurora's name," I said.

"I suppose that's very true. There's a lot to work out, but I feel OK about a lot more now."

"I had been worried that if you or I dated or slept with someone else, then we'd never get back together and that we'd lose what we had."

"It never went away, but didn't you know that last night?"

"I love you," I told him.

"You owe me a ring. I want and need to be tied to you in that sense."

"OK," I said.

I didn't ask him why he changed his mind, or what had happened to his sensible slow-and-steady approach to our relationship. I had known all along that he'd give in. In the battle between love and logic, love always wins.

7

Getting home is taking too long. I feel like I've been driving forever.

Still no text from Jay.

Murdock and Sandro spent most of tonight reminding me of the reasons I shouldn't get back together with Jay.

"But I love him," I said.

"Is that really enough?" Murdock asked.

"It will be."

I texted Jay to ask about his plans for later tonight. It's been more than a month since our last night together in his bedroom. I badly wanted to see him and kiss him.

"Brett is coming over to play Wii," he said. "But I'll see you tomorrow night for dinner."

"What dinner?" I asked.

"I thought we talked about it the other night," he said. "Let's have dinner tomorrow night and talk about everything."

I put down my phone.

"I asked him to hang out tonight, and he said no," I told Murdock and Sandro. "He's going to play Wii and get high."

"He told you that?" Sandro asked.

"He told me the Wii part. I'm assuming the weed part."

"And this is really the man you want to be with?" Murdock asked.

How do you fix something that has broken? Superglue and tape and other adhesives, but the thing you've broken is never the same. Fault lines, indicating where the fault lies. You fix things by lying, and in time the lies don't feel like lies anymore because these lies are all you know.

And I'm tired of lying.

He isn't giving me what I want, and his reasons are no longer good enough. Were never good enough, actually. I just refused to see what everyone else clearly can.

Jay hurt my feelings when he told me he didn't want to get together, and instead of agreeing that waiting until tomorrow would be just fine, I tried to hurt him the same way he had hurt me.

It made sense at the time.

"I think my children and I are going to pass on a relationship with you," I finally responded to him. "But I wish you nothing but the best. It's a Wii. I'm a person. As much as I love you, I deserve more. And I will find it."

That's when I left the bar, walked to my car in its fee-free parking spot in the South End, and drove home.

8

Holly and Avery are asleep. I'm sitting on the couch that is my bed, and I'm drinking some water.

I had what I thought I wanted. I won him back. He came around. He forgave me. He knew all of my secrets and all of my lies and still loved me. No one has loved me the way he has. He was right about that, that afternoon I chased him into the parking lot. He sees me and still finds me beautiful.

And each time he doesn't give me what I want, I feel a little less like myself and more disposable, kind of. Does that make sense? I'm a toy he can take out of the box and play with when he wants to, but has no problem putting away when he isn't in the mood to play.

I expected him to reply to my text by asking what was wrong, since my response to him was clearly out of character, given how hard I've worked—not just this week but since the beginning, really—to cultivate and protect my relationship with him.

My phone lights up, signaling his response. I shut my eyes, make something of a wish, and then I turn over the phone to read his response.

"I can't deal with the mind games. I am done. Thank you for letting me see Avery one last time. Goodbye, Rabbit. I mean it fully this time. Please leave me alone. Do not call me again. Do not text. I seriously have a restraining order, and I will use it if you contact me again."

Then he texts a picture of the restraining order.

"I mean it. For your health and for mine, Rabbit, stay away from me."

"I'm sorry," I reply. "I'm wrong. I made a mistake."

I believe each of those things to be true, but I didn't just tear down our house; this time, I set it on fire, and the wall dividing East from West has been rebuilt stronger than it was when it was first erected.

I need a minute. I need to re-read the I love yous and you're the one and let's meet for ice cream and I'm sorry for making fun of you and Call me Will 2.0 and the pair of goodbyes that began it all.

I've come full circle, back to the beginning where he and I weren't talking and I was out of ideas for how to change that.

All of the things I could have done differently tonight. I should have stayed home with Holly. I shouldn't have ordered a drink. I should have told him that I was out with friends and would talk to him later. I shouldn't have responded the way I did. All of these I statements.

I turn out the lamp next to the couch, and I pull a blanket on top of me. We have more than taken on water—we have sunk.

No mermaid is strong enough to pull us from this wreckage.

Strands of Night and Fire

1

We return, pigeons and salmon, to the places we abandoned and to the place where we were abandoned. Our secrets, each of them, years worth, spill out of our mouths like rubies and other precious stones. Doesn't matter if there is no one around to hear our telling. We scatter those secrets like other broken things, fragile and winged. We wait for absolution much longer than we should. We bury our secrets. We forget our dead.

2

I have to sign the lease to the apartment. Holly is at work. Avery and I meet the owners of the home and their children. We walk through the apartment, and I take more pictures. Avery's patience impresses the landlord and his family. I can have the keys before the end of the month. New locks to install and floors to clean. Can I afford the rent and still pay child support? Don't know. Haven't paid child support before. But I think so.

"The apartment is mine," I tell Holly, when she gets home from work. She is tired, and her head hurts. She is feeling very pregnant, though Aurora isn't due for nearly five months. Holly is beginning to show. She goes to sleep early. I think our nights of drinking tea after Avery is asleep are over.

She looks at the pictures and says the apartment looks lovely.

Holly never uses the word lovely.

Eleven hours ago, and then more than 11 hours ago, Jay reminded me about a dinner we won't have.

3

"I ruined everything again," I say to Kathy. We were already scheduled to meet today. "All I needed to do was let him have one night. That's all he wanted."

"Until next week, when he would have asked for a second night, and then a third. Don't you see? He was never going to give you what you wanted. You can't make him healthy. You can't make him the right one for you. He is not the right one for you."

That's as much as she wants to talk about it, this psychiatrist who worried that I would relapse and prescribed me medication that might make my skin fall off.

"He forgave me. He knew everything, and he still loved me."

"Is love telling you not to come over because I'm going to get high? Is love using in the first place? I don't think love is either of those things, and I think you don't either. You saw what was happening. You protected yourself. You did nothing wrong."

"Everything was wrong."

"Do you hear yourself? He makes you not healthy. Stay away from him. He is not right for you."

"I love him."

"And then you won't. That's what will happen. You love him now. You won't love him later."

I make a follow-up appointment for two weeks from now. Kathy thinks seeing me again that soon is for the best.

"Don't relapse," she cautions, when she walks me to the receptionist. "And think about why his not wanting to hang out affected you as much as it did. There's something to that."

She adds to her list of recommendations: Keep taking the Lamictal. Find ways to distract myself. Keep the appointment with the therapist. Call if I need to talk about anything.

4

We've all had our hearts broken. You have to start counting days since you last saw, touched, kissed, loved the man or woman who broke your heart. Start at zero. There's likely an app that breaks days down into more manageable accomplishments. Hours. Minutes. Seconds. Then longer periods. Weeks. Months. Years.

People fake forget until they for-real forget. They wear rubber bands around their wrists to help break a bad habit. When they think about the habit—the person or the activity—or when they engage in the behavior, they snap the rubber band, which trains their mind to link the habit with pain. Pain as reinforcement. Touching and re-touching a stove hot enough to peel and blister skin. Similar to, but not quite like, cutting.

5

"I'm sorry for all of this," I say to Holly. I've lost track of the number of ways I've told her the same thing. The apologies piled in front of her like candles, each lit with an unspoken promise to not do it again.

6

Days three and four are failures. If getting over someone is like dieting, then I've used a month's worth of cheat days before losing a pound. Yoga helps, and I'm finding a kind of solace in spending an hour, sometimes two, on the treadmill. Up to 4.8 miles in an hour, and I can almost fit into medium tank tops. Down a pants size. Failures, days three and four, which means I'm back to zero. Start counting days since I last saw, touched, kissed, loved Jay.

7

The universe, with her wicked humor and blue-green laugh, pleased with herself. The last name of the therapist Erin selected is Locke. So I'm seeing a lock to deal with my missing key. I put the key to his childhood bedroom, and its chain, in an envelope. The envelope I've put in a box, one of a few I've brought home to use during my move. I'll need more.

After taking a family history, and getting some basic information, including how much my insurance will pay, Jean asks me to start at the beginning and go from there. We have an hour, she says. Take my time.

The Wurlitzer organ signals the start of the ride. I've selected a thoroughbred this go-around. Ignore the rabbits; they're nothing but trouble. A frog and toad in front of me, a tiger and lion behind. The carousel is safe, only as fast as it is programmed to be. My thoughts, currently tamed by medication, let loose to run.

The website, and the first date, and the drugs, then the recording and the suicide attempts and my stay at St. Elizabeth's. The proposal and the party and the day he met Avery; then this week of text messages and what I found there.

"He wasn't the only addict," she says. "You were just as addicted, but to the possibility of him. You had been living a lie. You did not know how to have a healthy relationship with him because he is not healthy. You were constantly reacting to what he did and said instead of just being with him."

"He's been hurt before. He said he loved me more than he has ever loved anyone. And I hurt him. I was careless with him. If I had been better able to help him, or if I had known how to help him, then he and I would still be together."

"You're spending too much time talking about him and not enough time talking about yourself," Jean says.

"But how I was with him is who I am."

"You were a version of yourself with him, but you were not you. You can't be hung up on someone who is no longer an option. If you don't take care of your emotional needs, you will continue attracting men who don't take care of their emotional needs and are unable to take care of your emotional needs as well. He took advantage of a weakness he saw in you."

"A weakness?"

"You had a void. He recognized it because he has a similar void in himself. He knew he could get from you what he needed. He manipulated you."

"I don't think that's true." I say. "I don't have a void."

"Then who are you?"

"I'm a single father. I'm a husband, barely. I'm a friend."

"Don't tell me who you are in relation to everyone else. Who are you?"

"I don't know who I am separate from who I am with other people."

"That's right. You don't know who you are. You're afraid of people not wanting you, and afraid of people leaving you, so you pick people who will never work out so that the outcome is that they leave you or don't pick you. They walk away from you. That's the cycle. You play out the one thing you don't want to happen just to prove yourself right. And then it happens and you wonder why."

"Nobody wants to be rejected," I say. "No one wants to be left behind."

"Then break the cycle. And if you don't think you're ready to break the cycle, then ask yourself why. You're the only one standing in your way."

"I am not standing in my way. I don't want to feel what I feel anymore. I don't want to feel, if the only thing I'm feeling is hurt. I love him. I thought he was the one."

"You picked someone you couldn't end up with," Jean says.

"I lied to him about being married. I led him on. He fell in love with me. I wasn't available. But I thought I would be available."

"He's a drug addict. He wasn't and isn't available."

155

"But he didn't lie."

"All addicts lie, Will. The pills?"

She's good, I think. She pays attention, and she listened to me, even when I felt like I was leaving out important details and that the story wasn't coming out right.

"He said it was only that one time."

"Wasn't that one time one time too many?"

"I loved him enough to risk our relationship."

"And you lost him to his addiction. There was no getting him back. Even if you had been single and available for a relationship with him, you wouldn't have gotten it. You and he developed an unhealthy co-dependency. You thought you could fix him. He liked that you took care of him."

"I miss him," I say.

"Moving on is the best thing you can do, because otherwise you will get stuck."

"I am stuck. How will I find someone else who will love me and my kids?"

"Thinking you can move past him and this experience by jumping into the first relationship that presents itself, or that you think you can make work, is co-dependent thinking."

"What's the difference between co-dependency and love?"

"When you don't have to ask me that, then you'll know what the difference is."

Would anything be different if Jean had been able to see me last week? Thinking so is a bit like blaming her for things going wrong, though.

Don't count the days I talk to Jean about Jay. I have to talk to Jean about Jay. Part of the process. So these days

156

don't count. And if I'm going to succeed, then I have to allow some room for him. A picture developed in reverse. Image to negative to camera click. Nothing left to expose. Everything out on the table.

Jean suggests distractions are in order, as is finding other support systems. Groups out there, for people like me.

"Gay?" I ask.

"Struggling," she counters.

8

After work, I get the keys to my new apartment. Halfway between Holly and where Jay lives. Damn. The invisible rubber band snapping against my wrist. The apartment is empty. The books will take the longest to move. Ten bookshelves. Six shelves. Each shelf double-stacked with books. Holly picked out about forty books that she wants; I'm taking the rest.

I move them over in boxes, one bookshelf at a time. Holly and I agree to throw out the old bookshelves. I'll buy new ones. She'll put them together. She's always put together our bookshelves. Easier, I think, putting together something from scratch than reassembling something you've had to take apart. No real rush, since Holly isn't going anywhere.

I pack my clothes and find the scarf Jay—snap—wrapped around my neck during our second date.

"Are you going to keep the scarf?" Holly asks.

"I'll use it this winter."

But the rest of what he gave Holly to give to me, and everything of his I didn't return, I put in a box that I label Emotional Baggage: Do not open.

I put the box on a shelf in a closet in my bedroom, and by the time I've finished moving into my apartment, I've stacked other boxes in front of it.

Avery begins spending two or three nights a week with me. He has his side of the bed, and I have my side, and he helps me make the bed in the morning.

But before he wakes up—or, more accurately, before I wake him up—I sit in front of my computer and I look for e-mails that don't come and I Google phrases like "What becomes of the brokenhearted" and "Healing a broken heart."

Thousands of hits returned in less than one second. Remedies and reasons and retribution.

Gradually, I yield to the fact that Jay is no longer part of my life, and that Holly and I no longer live together. But our lives remain entwined, not just because of Avery and Aurora, but because she and I have shared too much to just let each other go. We have dinner together several nights each week. We text when things go well at work and when things don't go well. She remains the person I tell things to when I have things to tell.

And truth be told, I think she's secretly happy all of this happened.

"I'm sad for us, but I'm also relieved," she says. "We don't have to pretend anymore. Aren't you relieved?"

"I just feel really lost. Not unsafe; just lost."

"You may for a while, but not forever."

"I don't like it."

"I know, but this is part of the journey. It is the journey."

Holly and I, relating to each other the way we've always related to each other. Advice. Suggestions.

Comfort. You'd think we'd be different, if different is the right word. I betrayed her. I was going to leave her.

Five months pregnant, then five-and-a-half months pregnant. Aurora is the size of a blueberry, a plum, a head of lettuce, then bigger. She has ears and a nose and a mouth. She sucks her thumb; she turns somersaults.

And Holly, on her bed now, talking about how difficult getting over Jay is.

How's the weather? What's for dinner? I'm still in love with him.

"I just don't want to be sad. I don't want to think that I really fucked up," I say. "I don't want to think that I'll think about it and him forever. I don't want to think this is all my fault."

"Nothing is your fault. You made decisions. There were consequences. You are in the birthing process of a new and better life."

"I need an epidural," I say.

Holly laughs.

"He always said that moving on would be easy," I say. "But if he moves on, then he and I will never get a chance to make it right."

"Maybe he has moved on," Holly says. "Instead of working on himself, he's throwing himself into another relationship. What will that do for him? Maybe he's escaping even further into drugs. Did you want that? Do you want that? Will it make you feel better to know that if you and he had gotten back together I would have taken out a restraining order against him? I would never have let him raise my children. Then what would you have done? What would you have picked? The kids or him?"

"The kids," I say. "No question."

"That certainty you feel about them is how he feels about drugs," she says.

9

Another morning in front of the computer, and I find, and read, and then re-read, an eleven-page PDF abstract of a 200-page document called "The Long-Term Worldwide Effects of Multiple Nuclear Weapons Detonations."

Long-term worldwide effects.

Multiple nuclear weapons detonations.

So, something worse than my relationship with Jay ending.

Explosions in the sky and in the ground and in the world that Holly and I built. Long-term worldwide effects. Ripples and ripples and ripples again.

During the partial-hospital program, Erin said that hearts are muscles. To build muscle, you have to break down what you have, so it can rebuild itself bigger and stronger.

Broken hearts are just waiting for the right reason to be fixed. Or she said something like broken hearts are just waiting for the right reason to be fixed. I wasn't fully listening to Erin, when she talked about broken hearts, convinced that my heart would not be broken for long. He'd come around, I thought. Give him time.

After becoming kings and queens, the Pevensie siblings, Peter, Susan, Edmund, and Lucy, return through the wardrobe, children again.

Frodo Baggins and Samwise Gangee see the ring destroyed in a fire of lava. Ariel gets back her voice. True love's kiss wakes up sleeping beauty.

The glass slipper fits Cinderella's foot. Harry, Hermione, and Ron survive the Battle of Hogwarts.

To return from her adventures on the other side of the looking glass, and from her journey through Wonderland, Alice has to wake up.

10

Holly and I take turns making family dinner. One night, Holly says "feel, here, something hard," and I touch her stomach and I feel what can only be a heel or an elbow. I push into Holly and Aurora kicks or punches back. She starts turning in circles inside Holly. Holly laughs and I laugh and I push into Holly's stomach and Avery sees what I'm doing and he pushes my hand away and he kisses Holly's stomach and says "my baby."

"Do you know your sister is in here?" I ask.

"Yes," Avery says.

"Do you know you were in here?"

"Yes."

"What was it like?" I ask, knowing that Avery can't remember what growing inside of Holly was like, but that he will try to find the right words to describe what he can't remember.

"Was it cozy?" Holly asks.

"Yes," Avery says. "Cozy."

The three of us—soon to be four—remain a family, because families do not break; they simply untangle and rearrange.

11

I've told some people what happened. They were more understanding than I expected. One found a gay dads' support group for me to try. It meets twice a month at a church that is about a half hour from my home. The men in the group are going through, or have survived, bitter divorces with women who do not understand why their husbands are now gay.

Now gay, these men say, and they laugh. As if being or not being gay is a choice.

Six men sitting in a circle. The basement of a church. Thirty miles from my apartment. Didn't know they expected a five-dollar contribution for being there. I didn't bring money. Pay double next time, the group leader says.

Won't be coming back, I don't say, though I already know, even before saying anything to these six men sitting in a circle in the basement of a church.

Metal folding chairs. Cold coffee. The way these men talk to each other with a familiarity I'm no longer interested in having.

"Holly and I will not have a bitter divorce," I say.

"Give it time," one man says.

After the group ends, but before I can leave, one man explains that he and his wife used fertility treatments in order to conceive. Three years, the two of them tried, until they were successful. Twins.

This guy, now gay, sees his twins once a month.

I call Holly after the meeting, and I tell her what these men went through or are going through. I tell Holly what I told the men, that she and I would not be evil and vindictive.

"I hope not," Holly says. Then she asks if I'm planning to go back.

"I don't think so," I say. "It's kind of far from home, and I don't think I got anything out of it."

The next night, I attend an Alanon meeting for gay men and lesbians who have been affected by someone's drug or alcohol addiction. Another church basement. More metal folding chairs. More coffee.

I listen to the stories, and I recognize myself. When I'm asked to share, because all new people have to at least share their first name and a little about what brought them, I say just enough to see recognition and sympathy. Not anything anyone says, more in the way their bodies shift, and after, while drinking a cup of coffee, three men come and ask how I'm doing and if I've talked to the man again. I didn't use Jay's name. Just called him my ex-boyfriend.

I join an online support group for men and women who failed to kill themselves. No. That's not what I'm supposed to say. Who succeeded at living. That's the way we wrap up our stories of desperation and despair. Succeeded at living. Tie a ribbon around that package. Inside is a mostly empty box.

Yoga keeps me grounded, as does time on the treadmill. My body is changing. Growing smaller.

I practice six days a week. Plank to downward dog to the three warriors to pigeon to crow to standing balances. Avery has started mimicking some of the poses at home. He knows the poses by their names. Holly and I are looking for a daddy-and-me yoga class.

Once I conquer crow, I start working on a headstand.

"This position is important," the instructor says, "because it puts your heart above your head."

Love over logic.

I am in downward dog, and the instructor asks us to turn our head to the left and then the right. Facing left, I see the red EXIT sign above the door. The sign has always been there, and yet I feel like I'm seeing the sign for the first time.

I read the sign as EX-IT. Ex it.

I am Jay's ex-it.

I chose not to see the signs.

After class, the instructor tells me that of all of the students, I'm the bravest.

"Why?" I ask.

"You're not afraid to fall."

A Matter of Speculation

1

I am awake, but Avery is asleep. I untangle my body from his and walk into the kitchen. I've already set up coffee for the morning, and I turn on the machine. I hear the sound coffee makes when it brews and then drips into a glass pot. These rare nights now when I can't sleep give me the chance to consider everything happening around me. Aurora. How Holly and I have transitioned into living in two homes. How Avery has taken to it, bringing with him between houses a bag of toys. Likely gives him a sense of stability, Jean, who I still see once a week, says about Avery's bag of toys. Already, Avery pits me against Holly. She gives in more often than I do, though I'm more flexible on the things that she isn't. We've found equilibrium. The pendulum no longer swings over a pit. No one is speaking from inside the walls.

A sky streaked in reds and yellows, then more light inside. Avery, still asleep, filled with secrets and mysteries. Sometimes he sits up, asks for something to drink, and by the time I've brought him a cup of water, he is on his back, eyes closed. I don't think he actually wakes up. I think he's just making sure I'm still there.

We resume walking around the Charles River on Saturdays and Sundays. Sometimes I stop at a Starbucks and order Avery a box of vanilla milk. I haven't run into anyone who knew me with Jay. Don't think I will. We are not orbited by the same groups of people, though I think we will occasionally find ourselves at the same events. There's the Ani DiFranco concert in a couple of months. I'll see him again there. Won't talk to him. Don't want to be escorted out for being within 200 feet of him. That restraining order continues to tie me to him. It should never have been issued. The judge just didn't have all of the facts.

Holly calls out of work sick one Saturday, and she asks to spend the day with Avery. I cede my time with Avery, since Holly gets him so seldom on weekends. I skip walking at the Charles River, but take a book and a blanket to the Public Gardens.

I walk from Boston Common through the Public Gardens and back again. Along these paths, Jay and I chased Avery one weekend; along these paths I walked the day Jay found the phone, and the day he and I ordered ice cream with Avery. Those earlier versions of me likely wouldn't recognize this man walking along the paths, alone.

I watch men disassemble the carousel erected six months ago in the middle of Boston Common. The men lift horses, rabbits, and frogs off their poles and pack them away in crates filled with hay.

The white rabbit is taken off its pole last. The men lower it into a box and screw on a lid.

I watch the men dismantle the carousel and pack away the animals and the lights and the seats and the ticket booth.

I am witness to the onset of hibernation.

These same men will resurrect the carousel next summer. Avery will be one year older, Aurora will be too young to ride, and I will bring Avery back to the carousel and watch him choose his animal and hold on as if his life depends on it, because I will make sure he knows that his life depends on it.

In these flash-forwards, I do not see anyone standing with me, holding Aurora, taking pictures of Avery and me on the carousel. In these flash-forwards, I am always walking the paths in Boston Common and the Public Gardens alone. I try to imagine someone walking with me, but the only person I want to be there is no longer an option.

I took a picture of this carousel the night Jay and I were together on Newbury Street. The picture is still on my phone. I still haven't deleted photographs from my time with him, or our last week of text messages. I haven't re-read them, but I like knowing that they are there, in case I want to re-read about the time when someone loved me.

2

During our eighth session, Jean asks what I'm going to do about the restraining order.

"I can't do anything," I say. "There will be a hearing next year, and I'll show up for that one."

"I think you should try to move that hearing date up," she says. "If you don't, you're going to spend the next year thinking about it, and that isn't going to be good for you."

"I'm not sure what I can do," I say.

"I think you need to find out," she says.

I agree, but I do nothing at first, convinced that there is nothing I can do. But the more I think about it, the more I think Jean is right, and only after a series of unrelated events do I decide to see what options I have.

I went to a concert, and even though he never expressed interest in the band, I knew that if he was there, he'd have no problem using the restraining order to have me removed.

I go on a date at a restaurant close enough to where he lives that he could be there. And I think that if he was there, or walked by and saw me, he could call the police and use the restraining order to end my date.

And Holly thinks Jay is crazy enough to use the restraining order, even if I've done nothing to violate it.

"You don't know what he's capable of," she says.

But I know what Jay is capable of. I know the stories of his previous relationships.

I don't want him to want to use the restraining order. I want him to miss me and want to know how I'm doing and one day meet for a cup of coffee.

"You're still grieving," Jean says. "You're still somewhere between denial and acceptance."

"Not acceptance," I tell her. "I want him back, and I think he'll come back."

"You don't want him back," she tells me.

"I'm lonely."

"You won't be forever," she says.

But I am, and at night, I go online and seek out men who live nearby who are also lonely and looking. I tell these men what I'm willing to do with and to them, and what I'm not willing to do. And these men respect my boundaries.

I've had sex with more than one dozen men in the last few weeks. None of them anything special; sometimes I just want to be needed.

Distractions, Jean said. She told me to find distractions.

She doesn't tell me if she thinks I'm making poor decisions.

My friends do. They're tired of waiting for whatever is coming to come. Surely something big is coming, or the story would have ended with his last text message. That night, I thought the story had ended, but then I woke up on Sunday, and on Monday, and on Tuesday, and each day since.

Turns out the story isn't the story of my time with Jay but is really the story of my time without Jay. And maybe even me without Holly.

I'm stuck in this post-break-up zone, which is complicated by the nature of the relationship and the nature of the seismic shifts in my life.

But I'm OK. Really, I am. I'm better. I'm healing. I've healed.

Bullshit, a friend at work says. When you don't have to say how healthy you are, then you'll be healthy. Until then, needing to say I'm OK is the same as saying I'm not OK.

3

"You don't need to rush into anything," Kathy says. "Take your time. No one is grading you on how you're doing."

She and I no longer dance through these sessions, taking steps toward and away from some heady realization about life and the universe and all that.

Instead, we use our now-monthly check-ins to talk about how I feel on the medication and if I think it is still working.

"I just don't want to hurt."

"In time, you won't," she says.

The right side of her mouth turns up a little, and I think she feels sorry for me.

I don't want my psychiatrist feeling sorry for me.

"So any racing thoughts? Alcohol? Depression? Any contact with him? How is Holly? How is your son handling living in two houses?"

Kathy still has the same folder she started on me at St. Elizabeth's. We check in and she writes me a prescription.

"Are you feeling unwell?" she asks.

She always says *unwell*. She never asks if I'm feeling *sick*.

"No," I say—I always say— "I'm feeling fine."

"Are you lonely?" she asks.

"No."

"Good," Kathy says. "That's good."

Jean asks similar questions during our sessions. We don't meet every week now. Every other week for the next two months. Then once a month. Then maybe not at all.

She thinks I should start dating. No commitment beyond one date. Get to know myself in relation to other people.

"I don't think I've ever really dated," I say.

"Don't you think it's time you do?"

I don't until I do, and I do until I don't, and you may think that I can't feel both as strongly as I do but I feel all of it. I want to move on but I don't want to want to move on because moving on—fully moving on and being open

170

to the possibility of a relationship—means he's no longer an option.

I gave up counting days. He's part of me. Not thinking about him is impossible.

And then I'm on my way home after work one evening, and I see him. He's driving a car he must have bought. He's at a red light that is perpendicular to the red light I've stopped in front of. I recognize his earrings before I recognize his face.

Seeing him outside of my dreams is surprising. I don't dream about him every night, but often enough to sometimes look for him, if I'm conscious enough in my dreams to think that I should look for him. Sometimes we're fucking. Sometimes I'm reading a magazine on the couch and he's making dinner.

He's laughing at something I've said.

He's explaining the way a helicopter works to Avery. Hand gestures. Sound effects. Spinning in circles with Avery until Avery asks to be let down. Dizzy. Rest a minute.

He's asking me if I remember when we weren't talking, and he's saying that those were some of the hardest months of his life.

I wake up from these dreams, and if we've been fucking, I'm hard, and if we haven't been fucking and if we've just been together, I wonder if I'm dreaming him or if he's dreaming me and if the connection we forged is still there.

His red light changes to green first, and he has to pass directly in front of me. He is looking forward and doesn't turn in my direction. He is scowling, and I think he is scowling because he saw me, or maybe because his boss is still a bitch and he doesn't know how long he can put up with working with her.

I can't tell Holly what color Jay's car is or its make and model. The only detail I can give her is that there is a crooked bumper sticker on his bumper.

"His life continued well without me in it," I say. "He doesn't miss me and Avery. He doesn't wonder if I think about him. He just moved on. He said he would."

"You don't know what he's feeling or doing, Will," she says. "And he's not your concern anymore."

"What if he's already moved on and found someone else to love?"

"I think he loves—or loved—you very much," Holly says. "I think because of how much he loved you, he acted toward you in the end the way he did."

"I don't know," I say.

"You know, I don't think about him as a person," Holly says. "He was a catalyst. You needed him in order to become you."

"Does *catalysis* have to hurt so much?"

"You had misery and unhappiness disorder."

"That's not a real disorder."

"Doesn't mean you didn't have it," Holly says.

I tell Jean during one of our sessions that I think that each day that passes takes me one day closer to the next *we* I'm meant to be a part of.

"Will, your next *we* may not be your final *we*. You may go through several *wes* before you find your final *we*."

I think she uses words like "final we" because I use words like "final we."

"I'm afraid of being hurt again."

"I think you're afraid of not being able to say goodbye."

172

"What do you mean?"

"You didn't get to say goodbye to him. He made that impossible. He took away your choice. And that's why you held on as tightly as you did, and why the end of the relationship triggered so much for you. It wasn't him that triggered you; it was what you didn't get to do or say."

"If I had just done something different or better, if I had been someone different or better, then he wouldn't have left me and I wouldn't be here and my heart wouldn't have broken," I say.

"You knew things were about to end," she says. "You didn't think he thought you were good enough, so you acted out in order to get him to tell you that you were good enough. You weren't getting what you wanted. He wasn't going to give it to you. You bugged his room. You weren't sleeping. You weren't eating. Those aren't normal behaviors in a healthy relationship. He didn't pick you, and he kept not picking you. And he still isn't picking you. It's time to move on. I think you know it's time to move on."

Without hands on a clock, you'll never know how long you've been stuck.

4

Holly, Avery, and I are at the courthouse where Jay took out the restraining order. I have to file a motion asking the judge to reconsider his decision, and in my motion I need to list my reasons for why the restraining order should never have issued. Holly tells me to be honest. Say everything, which includes leaving the phone in Jay's room. Up to the judge now. A clerk will send Jay notice of the hearing. It is scheduled for ten days from now. We'll need to find a babysitter, since Holly has agreed to come with me. A pregnant wife, as outraged as I am, should play well during the hearing.

A friend suggests I hire an attorney.

"Why?" I ask this friend, an attorney, though not skilled in this kind of law to offer representation.

"You need all the help you can get," she says. "An attorney will know how to best represent your side, and a judge is likely to listen more closely to an attorney than he will to you."

"Jay won't hire an attorney," I say. "He can't afford it."

"All the better for you," my friend says, though she cautions that getting a restraining order revoked, more than a month after it was issued, will not be easy. "Don't get your hopes up. It's likely the judge will leave it in place."

"Which means what?"

"It'll be on your record, and a future employer can learn about it during a typical background check."

"For the year it's in place?"

"It'll always be there," my friend says.

Jay and his restraining order, an incurable sexually transmitted disease.

The attorney I hire is sympathetic, though more to Holly than to me. She comes with me to meet with the attorney and his assistant, who will do most of the work, and this attorney, an overweight man with two children and a wife of twenty-two years he tells me, asks Holly what she will say, if asked to testify on my behalf.

"Is Will violent?"

"No."

"Has he ever hit you? Threatened you? Made you feel unsafe?"

"No," Holly says. Her belly has swelled enough that she needs to wear maternity clothes. She likes maternity clothes; the elastic waistbands make her feel thin, even at six months pregnant. She carries her weight in her tummy.

"And you'll write an affidavit attesting to these things?"

"Yes."

"You know you have that wife who is one in a million," the attorney says to me.

"I know," I say. I reach for Holly's hand, and she holds mine for a minute before letting it go.

"I have to go to a doctor's appointment," Holly says. "Is that all right?"

"I'll e-mail you a statement," the attorney says. "Print it, sign it, and bring it to our hearing next week."

After Holly leaves, the attorney takes my copies of the text messages Jay and I exchanged after the restraining order was in place. Proof, I think, that he does not feel threatened by me.

"Not many women would sit next to a husband who is defending himself against a restraining order filed against him by his ex-boyfriend."

"I know."

The attorney sends Holly and me our affidavits the day before our hearing. Affidavits are lists of numbered facts, truths that the undersigned believes. Each truth, a factor why the restraining order should be revoked. I read each fact and I wonder how things filled with hope end up empty sentences on pieces of paper, facts stacked together to convince someone that I am not a threat.

And then the last fact: On August 21, 2010, Jay texted me "I know you're it. My it. Us. You, me, Holly, Avery, and Aurora." "We can and we will get there." "I'm yours." "You're mine, Rabbit."

Yours. Mine. Ours.

"I can't believe the fact that he called me Rabbit is going to be part of the public record," I say to Holly.

"That is kind of funny," Holly says.

"Should I be doing this?"

"He didn't care about what the restraining order would do to you and your life. You have to do this to protect yourself and get your life back."

Too late to back out, but I want someone to tell me that I've made the right decision. I still need validation, which Jean and I have taken to talking about during our sessions.

5

Holly needs help climbing the steep stairs leading from the sidewalk to the courthouse where Jay and will appear before a judge. Holly reaches for my hand, albeit mostly out of habit, I think. I hold the door open for Holly. A guard waves us through the metal detector. He seems bored. Holly is holding my left hand.

"Have I ruined my future by losing him?" I ask her.

"He wasn't the one for you," she says. "He isn't the one for you."

Holly and I sit on a bench. My attorney texts to say he will be a few minutes late. Jay isn't here, and then he is here. He walks into the courthouse, and he is alone. He's carrying an envelope and several pages of notebook paper. I'm surprised Jay came alone. I expected him to bring Brett or Tyrese.

"There he is," I say to Holly.

And then my attorney arrives. He passes Jay, who is standing near a stairwell.

"We're on the third floor," my attorney says.

"He's here," I say, nodding in Jay's direction.

Holly and I walk up the stairs, my attorney follows, and behind him, Jay walks.

How surreal, all of this, I think.

My attorney points to a bench and tells Holly and me to sit. My attorney introduces himself to Jay.

"Can we talk?" I hear my attorney ask Jay.

Jay says yes.

I do not want to hear what Jay says. If I look at Jay, I will cry, and if I cry, then he will know that my heart continues to break, and that the heart he gave back to me is not the same heart I gave to him.

Holly squeezes my hand.

"Aurora is moving," Holly says. She puts my hand on her stomach. I feel Aurora kick.

My attorney comes back.

"He has agreed to vacate the restraining order, but he wants both of you to sign an order of non-trespass banning you from his home and where he works," my attorney says. "I don't think he's really authorized to ban you from the store, though."

"If that's what he needs, we'll sign it."

"He says you followed him into a parking lot once."

Followed him into a parking lot. Sometimes I should just shut up and get in the car. Thank you for that, Rabbit. I think we have a real relationship. I think we do both sides well. Father's Day weekend. The card ripped into confetti-sized pieces.

"I'll have to write up the order," my attorney says.

My attorney leaves to talk to Jay.

I know Holly wants to know how I'm feeling, but she isn't asking, and I don't feel like telling.

My attorney comes back to where Holly and I are still sitting.

"He wants you to write the statement," my attorney says to me. "He wants you to have no question what he is asking for and what you are agreeing to."

"Fine," I say.

I don't mind signing what Jay wants me to sign because I think he will move. He routinely picks up and goes once he has exploded his life.

I think about the ex-boyfriends Jay told me about, and I think that these ex-boyfriends are my brothers. They survived Jay; I will too. Line us up as we were at the end of our separate relationships with Jay, and I think we would each have the same haunted look in our eyes.

"He wants someone other than me to notarize the order," my attorney says. While the clerk looks for a notary, my attorney tells me what Jay had told him. "He feels very betrayed by you, and he needs no contact in order to heal. There's nothing left for you with him, just in case you weren't sure."

"I know," I say.

"Focus on your family," my attorney says.

A notary comes. Holly and I sign the order, and, once the order is notarized, go into the courtroom where the judge will vacate the restraining order.

Jay walks into the courtroom and sits on the opposite side of the room. He is crying.

"Are you OK?" Holly asks.

"I will be," I say.

The judge calls two cases before ours. A woman wants her boyfriend to stay away from her and stop bothering her family. The judge rules in her favor. A woman wants a restraining order against a man who could be her boyfriend, or her fiancé, and since he has not shown up, the judge rules in her favor. I think that this was Jay two months ago.

Betrayed, Jay had told my attorney.

The judge calls our case. Jay and I approach the judge, and my attorney stands with me.

The judge asks for our names. Jay gives his; I give mine; my attorney says his. The clerk asks us to raise our right hands and solemnly swear to tell the truth, the whole truth, and nothing but the truth. Jay says yes, and I say I do.

Not quite the *I do* I thought I'd offer Jay.

"Did you agree to vacate the restraining order on your own accord?" the judge asks Jay, who nods, "and do you know that you can come back about this, even if the order is vacated?"

"I do," Jay says.

There is his *I do*.

The judge nods and bangs his gavel. The restraining order is vacated.

All of this feels anti-climactic. I wanted the chance to tell my side. I wanted to tell the judge that Jay is a drug addict. I wanted the judge to order Jay to complete rehab.

I still wanted to save him.

Jay leaves quickly. He doesn't look at Holly and me.

Holly and I wait for a copy of the vacated restraining order, and then we leave.

I drive less than three blocks before I start to cry. Holly starts crying too. I know she is crying because I am crying about Jay.

"Do you think I will ever love again?" I ask.

"Yes," Holly says.

"Will I ever find a man as beautiful as he is?"

"You shouldn't be thinking about finding your next boyfriend. Focus on yourself. And when you find him, focus instead on his inner beauty. Outer beauty fades. But really, have you ever dated someone who wasn't beautiful?"

"What if he was the one and I totally fucked it up?"

"Will, if he was the one, he wouldn't have taken out the restraining order, and you wouldn't have been here in the first place. He wasn't your one. But you will find him."

"I hope so," I say.

I've stopped crying, because it is unfair to Holly.

"Don't hope," she says; "know."

I'm fluent in a dead language. He has scars on his arms and a tattoo of Buddha on his back. Lights candles when he drinks wine. Sometimes falls asleep during movies. Eats lemons and avocados whole. Paints his toenails with clear polish. Wears argyle socks and wife-beater tank tops.

Bird Girls with Hollow Bones

1

One Saturday afternoon, when he sees that I've been crying, Avery asks if I am sad.

Avery holds my right hand, turns it over, and then does the same to my left hand. He looks at my face and my arms. If I'm sad, then I must be hurt, and if I'm hurt, then I must be bleeding.

A three-year-old boy's logic.

"Where?" he asks.

"My heart," I say.

"Oh," he says. He shrugs his shoulder. He doesn't know where my heart is.

"Don't be sad, Daddy," Avery says. Then he kisses me. Sloppy kisses on my mouth and my nose and my cheeks and my forehead.

I'm sad today because I miss Jay, not my boyfriend Jay, but the Jay I met who, on our first date, took off his shirt because he was warm, and who played his flute—despite warning me that he hadn't played well in years—and the Jay who showed me YouTube videos of a bat flying around his bedroom.

I miss the Jay who, after I left the night of our first date, texted me lyrics from a Tori Amos song and made sure I knew that all he had to offer was mine for the taking.

Today, Jay would look through me as if I were glass.

"Do you need Mommy?" Avery asks.

"No, baby," I say.

"I need you, Daddy."

I start to cry harder.

Avery looks at me, and in all seriousness, says, "I pooped."

I want to laugh because his saying I pooped at this moment is funny, but I am still crying.

He runs into his bedroom, takes off his pants and diaper, and lies on the floor. I change him, and when I am done, he says, "Do you need Mommy now?"

"Yes, baby," I say, "I'll always need your Mommy."

"Let's go for a ride," I suggest, once Avery is wearing a clean diaper. I drive with no destination in mind, but end up at a cemetery about 15 miles away from my apartment. Crime scenes, each of these graves.

Avery likes the cemetery. When we come across a particularly steep section, he interlaces his fingers with mine, and I wonder how long he will let me hold his hand before he thinks holding his dad's hand is embarrassing, or that Holly and I are embarrassing.

He and I start going every Saturday after morning yoga. I pack a lunch for us and a change of clothes for him, and he and I walk down steep paths, and I count headstones and ask him to count as high as he can. He never asks what we're doing or why we're doing it. He's happy just being with me.

I recognize grief in cemeteries, a woman wearing black and holding flowers, and I recognize grief outside of cemeteries. A man in a grocery store, no list, putting items in his grocery cart that seem like the types of items to put in his grocery cart, a strip of pale skin on his left ring finger where once there was a ring; even Holly, sometimes, when she and I pass Avery back and forth.

And I also recognize the not-grief of cemeteries. We celebrate life in cemeteries, not death. We mourn, because we are taught to mourn. We buy flowers. We cry. We say he went too soon, or he is in a better place, or the pain got to be too much in the end.

Inside these cemeteries where Avery and I walk, are the people you learn about in sixth and seventh grade history class. Hazard of living in Massachusetts during the Revolutionary War; you became a footnote in a history book.

Louisa May Alcott's headstone and Ralph Waldo Emerson's headstone and Nathaniel Hawthorne's headstone. Pens and pads of paper and quarters and nickels and dimes. I have to ask Avery not to collect the change and put it in his pocket. Tempting fate, stealing from the dead. Bury your dead with pennies on their eyes so they can pay the ferryman.

Avery and I search for statues of angels in these cemeteries. There are several angels at Mount Auburn Cemetery and three in Concord, Massachusetts near the home where Louisa May Alcott wrote *Little Women*. Some of the angels have missing feathers; other angels have scars where pieces have eroded over the years. One angel at Mount Auburn is missing her nose. I touch the space where her nose was and it is cold. Granite is always cold.

I think all angels are women, even the angels who look like they are men. Avery doesn't know these women are angels. He calls these granite angels "birds," and then after he gets used to cemeteries and the game he thinks we're playing, he calls these granite angels "bird girls." Sometimes he stretches his arms away from his body and moves them up and down, mimicking flight, or wings, and I watch him and sometimes I have to squint because he is so beautiful.

"Two hands, Daddy," Avery says. "Hold Avery's hands with two hands."

I search for angels in cemeteries because after the big hole had been blown into my life, I started having these dreams that I was flying, and then my back began feeling like it was about to split open. The pain felt like a growing and breaking apart.

One morning, when it is cold enough to sleep under a down comforter, I wake up in a pool of feathers. The feathers had stretched their way out of the comforter. Emily Dickinson wrote that hope is a thing with feathers. How is a raven not like a writing desk? The raven has feathers.

Icarus had wings of wax. He flew until he didn't.

At the end, before I knew it was the end, when I thought it was just another beginning, I called him Icarus. Twice, via text message: "Icarus."

What was I thinking, daring him—us, really—to fall?

I wake up in a pool of feathers, and later that day, I am scheduled to see Jean.

"I feel something growing beneath my skin," I tell Jean.

"What do you think you feel?" she asks.

"Wings," I say.

"You're not growing wings," she says. "And you know you're not growing wings."

"I know," I say, "but I like thinking that I am growing wings."

Hope is a thing with feathers.

No wings, no hope.

"You should see your doctor about what you're feeling," Jean says.

If Jean knew what I'm not telling her, she would suggest she and I talk about what I'm not feeling, but I'm not sure how to talk about the *nots* in my life. Maybe later, once I've gotten a better handle on the *nows*.

"I'll make an appointment," I say, even though I'm most likely sore from practicing yoga five or six nights a week, and from putting in thirty-five miles a week on the treadmill. I continue to lose weight. I continue to get used to nights when Avery is with Holly and I am alone and the only sound in my apartment is the ticking of the clock I bought when I moved in.

Digital clocks don't need hands to tell time.

In cemeteries, Avery and I search for angels because they were put in place to remind us of someone who is missed, and when I find an angel, I touch it, and sometimes Avery spins in circles, and sometimes we spin in circles, and we laugh and we dance. I search for angels and I find them and I read the names and dates of the men and women and sometimes children buried beneath the angels' outstretched wings, and I wonder who picked out the angels.

The leaves start to turn. Another hazard of living in New England. Avery likes to pile these leaves in front of tombstones and jump into them. I help him, and he tosses these leaves in the air, and I toss these leaves in the air, and sometimes I toss him in the air, and I catch him and he laughs and above us angels smile or simply stare into space, blank. The leaves, when Avery jumps into them, crunch, just like ice and snow on a sidewalk in January.

185

Seasons in New England, one of my favorite parts about living here, especially how the changes are subtle until the changes are not subtle and you have no choice but to acknowledge what is no longer there while acknowledging what is there. Or what is left behind. Because left behind means something will be back. Winter to spring. Every year without fail.

Christmas lights are strung on houses before Thanksgiving in the neighborhood where I live. An electronic reindeer moves its head from side to side in front of one house. An inflatable Santa Claus is tied to a fence in front of another house.

"Lights, Daddy," Avery says. "Lights."

"What are the colors?" I ask, even though I know how well Avery knows his colors and how he can name the colors the right names every time. All these things he's learned when I was busy doing other things.

A Sunday at Mt. Auburn Cemetery and Avery is tired and will not walk. I do not bring his stroller on our cemetery walks.

"No more walk," he says. "Up, Daddy."

"In a minute," I say. "There's a bird girl."

I want him to want to walk because I don't feel like carrying him, and sometimes he will give in, but not today. He walks a few feet and stops.

"No more," he says.

He sits in front of a headstone. I sit with him. When he's willing to walk, we get up. I look at the headstone. I think it says Rabbit, but I look closer and see what I think is R is really an aged and weatherworn B. Babbit. Not rabbit.

2

Ticketmaster e-mails three hours before the Ani DiFranco concert that Jay and I have tickets for. Ani has postponed her Boston show.

Nine days after Ani DiFranco cancels her Boston concert, Ticketmaster sends another e-mail indicating that the event will not be rescheduled. The refund will happen automatically.

The concert is the only time I thought I might see him.

I wanted to see him, and I wanted him to want to see me.

I wanted to hear songs that meant something to him and to me.

I wanted him to see how much weight I've lost and how happy I am.

I wanted him to tell me hello.

I wanted to feel as if no time had passed.

3

Holly, Avery, and I celebrate Thanksgiving at my apartment. Avery falls asleep in the afternoon. I tell Holly I am grateful for her and for being alive. She says she's grateful for our rediscovered friendship.

We are in the kitchen, and I hug her from behind, and she stops what she is doing long enough to tilt her head into my shoulder. Familiar, the way our bodies fit, but not familiar at the same time, still learning how we fit.

Avery wakes up and is disoriented. He's peed his diaper and he asks to be changed. He and I play with cars and dinosaurs in the room where I have already set up a crib and where a bed in the shape of a car goes unused.

Avery refuses to sleep anywhere but in bed with me, when he is at my house, and in bed with Holly, when Avery is with her, and on nights like tonight, when Holly is staying the night, Avery asks for the three of us to sleep together.

"We don't do that anymore," Holly says.

And Avery understands enough to know that the three of us will not share a bed again. And Aurora will not know a time when she shared a bed with her parents. Her crib, blue, bought for Avery before Avery was born. He slept in the crib three or four times. Holly and I built that crib on a Sunday. We ate pizza. We watched a movie in which Sandra Bullock is slowly convinced that she is crazy. We went to bed late and talked about what life would be like once someone was sleeping in that blue crib.

Holly takes off a Saturday from work, and comes with Avery and me to Mount Auburn Cemetery. I point out angels to Holly and Avery, and Avery says "lady birds."

Holly laughs. Holly needs help walking up and down steep slopes. I hold her hand to help her. We do not interlace fingers. Her hand does not feel foreign in mine, but the way we hold hands has changed.

More than eight months pregnant. Wearing the biggest of her maternity clothes. The sun is bright on the snow on the ground, and Holly is wearing sunglasses.

The lake inside Mount Auburn Cemetery has frozen over, and on it, reflections of nearby trees and birds still flying south.

"Did you and that guy ever take Avery to a cemetery?" Holly asks.

Still, no one in my life says Jay's name.

"No," I say, "we didn't."

He would have, had I asked him to.

Two days later, Holly texts me at 7:50 a.m. Uncomfortable cramps. She's going to check in with her OB/GYN. Two hours later, she texts again: I'm five centimeters dilated. I'm in labor. Meet me at the hospital.

That walk with Holly and Avery, the last thing the three of us will do as a family of three.

Holly drives herself to the hospital. She has Avery. I leave work, drive to the hospital, and I worry that I'm driving so fast that I will be pulled over.

Holly and I get to the hospital at the same time. I take Avery to the woman who will watch him while we wait for Aurora to arrive.

"Is Mommy OK?" Avery asks.

"Yes," I say. "Your sister is coming."

Holly had told Avery already that his sister was on her way.

"Do you think she will like it here?" he asks.

"Absolutely."

"Do you think she will like me?"

"More than anyone else," I say.

I want to text Jay and tell him that I'm about to meet my daughter, but when I tell a friend what I feel, she tells me she will come to the hospital and take away my phone if I don't start focusing on my wife and our daughter.

When I get back to the hospital, Holly is still five centimeters dilated. Her water has not broken. In her room, a TV with the sound turned down. A resident examines Holly. We learn the doctor who will deliver Aurora is Dr. Yum. The resident asks if Holly wants her water manually broken or an epidural. Holly declines both.

"Aurora will come when she is ready," Holly says.

Holly and I are pros at labor and delivery.

At 9:15 p.m., the resident tells Holly that she can start to push. The resident pages the doctor, who arrives still putting on her scrubs. She is taking off her watch and wedding ring when Aurora's head crowns.

Dr. Yum is surprised at how quickly Aurora is arriving. The umbilical cord is loosely wrapped around Aurora's neck, but Dr. Yum slips it off. I am holding one of Holly's legs in the air, and a nurse is holding Holly's other leg.

"One more big push," the nurse says, and Holly pushes and tucks her chin into her chest and Aurora is born. 9:19 p.m.

Dr. Yum hands me a pair of surgical scissors and asks me to cut the cord, which I do. I hadn't been allowed to cut Avery's cord because the cord had been tightly wrapped around his neck. The resident takes Aurora to a warmer, where a NICU team is standing by to clean out her lungs and nose and make sure she is OK.

"What's going on?" I ask the nurse.

"Everything is fine," the nurse says, "but the birth happened so quickly that Aurora was stunned."

Aurora makes a noise, then she cries. I touch my daughter. I look at Holly and she is watching me and I know she is wondering if everything is OK. I know she is wondering if everything is OK because she and I do not need to talk to communicate. I nod at her, and she smiles.

"Do you want her on you?" the nurse asks Holly, and Holly says yes.

Aurora is brought to Holly, and she lowers the top half of her gown, and Aurora is put on Holly and immediately hunts for Holly's nipple. Aurora latches on and begins to suck.

The doctor and resident leave, and the NICU team leaves, and the nurses leave, and Holly and I are alone with Aurora, who continues to suck. Avery hadn't known how to latch for a few days, but Aurora, and Holly, know what to do.

She is here; my status update on Facebook.

I'm glad that Holly, Avery, and I had one last day together. Avery will not remember this cemetery walk, and in time, Holly and I may forget parts of this cemetery walk, but I have pictures. Holly, eight months pregnant, wearing sunglasses, and Avery walking between us, holding our hands, linking us together.

4

I learn some six months after the fact that Jay's mother is dead. I read and then re-read her obituary, and then I read and re-read his name as surviving her.

I think that I should have been there for him. I should have driven him to the airport and made sure he made his flights. I should have flown to Peoria, where his mother lived, because flying with him was my job.

He would search for the right words to say. He would keep from falling apart to keep others from falling apart.

Searched. Kept.

All of this happened months ago.

I call Holly, and when she answers and says hello, I can hear Aurora cooing, and I can hear that Avery is still awake, and Holly can hear that I'm upset.

"What's wrong?" she asks.

"His mother is dead."

"Did he get in touch with you?"

She doesn't have to ask who I'm talking about.

"No," I say. "I read the obituary online."

"I'm sorry," Holly says.

"Me too," I say. "I should have been there."

Holly is quiet, but the kids aren't, and I know she is tired, and I regret, not for the first time, that we don't live together. But I don't regret not living with her. If I lived with Holly, I wouldn't be able to do the things that I'm doing. And I like the things that I'm doing.

"There's nothing I can do," I say. "I hope the people in his life were able to comfort him and take care of him."

"That's the best you can hope for," Holly says.

I am quiet and trying not to cry, and Holly says she can stay on the phone as long as I need her to stay on the phone, but that she and the kids are tired.

I think she's afraid if she hangs up, I will call her from the bridge, and it will be July in December.

"OK," I say. "Thank you."

"Call me if you need me," she says.

"I will," I say.

Jay must feel like an orphan, I think. He and his sister will have to sift through their mother's belongings and decide what to keep. Sifting through his mother's belongings is what Jay expected he'd have to do.

Sifted. Past tense. Jay's mother has been dead six weeks and has already been cremated. Jay would have had to say something. He would have hated standing there, saying the things we're taught to say when someone we love dies.

After, he probably disengaged. He probably had to relearn how to breathe. He probably felt like he had to make sure everyone else could break down.

There's a man who lives near Peoria who I think Jay probably had sex with when he went home for the funeral. Jay and this man used to have sex, when Jay lived with his mom. I don't like thinking Jay and this man fucked.

Not much in the way of cards for condolences at the CVS near where I work. I don't put my return address on the card. He'll know the card is from me, and while I know he won't respond, at least I'll know that he knows I am thinking about him and hoping he is OK, even though he is probably not OK.

I put the card in an outgoing mailbox on the floor of the building where I work. A couple of hours later, on my way to a meeting, I walk by this box and it has been emptied.

5

People go to cemeteries because mothers and fathers and sisters and brothers and spouses and lovers and ex-lovers are buried in these cemeteries.

I don't mind when Avery loses interest in bird girls. I have no real reason left to mourn.

Besides, the weather has turned so cold that I don't want to play outside with Avery.

Indoors, Avery and I play, mostly dinosaurs. Sometimes he's the triceratops, and sometimes he's the tyrannosaurus rex, and sometimes he's a dinosaur that hasn't been discovered. I play the role of whatever dinosaur Avery wants me to be, even though I'd prefer to be the triceratops. I've always loved that three-horned herbivore.

"When can we play with Rora?" Avery asks.

"Soon she can play, and we will all be terrible lizards."

"No, Daddy," Avery says. "Aurora isn't a lizard. She's a baby."

"And what does that make you?"

"I'm the big boy. I'm your big boy, and you're daddy."

"And do you know how much I love you?"

"You love me this much," he says, spreading his arms as wide as his arms will spread.

"No," I say, "I love you this much."

I spread my arms as wide as my arms will spread, which is wider than how wide Avery's arms can spread.

"I love you, Daddy," Avery says.

"Who's my best friend?" I ask.

"Avery," he says. "Who's my best friend?"

"Daddy," I say.

Every time Avery and I have this conversation, which we have on the days and nights he and I are together, Avery hugs me after saying that I am his best friend, and I pick him up and hug him back until he tells me I am holding on too tight and he wants me to let him go.

Lost and Unclaimed Luggage Eventually Ends Up in Scottsboro, Alabama

1

With a man I'll never see again, I snuck back into St. Elizabeth's. We had been drinking coffee at my apartment when he asked me if I wanted to hunt light.

"Absolutely," I said.

"Care if we break the law?"

"Only if we're caught," I said.

He's an urban explorer. Breaking into places and waiting for light is what he does.

We got into St. Elizabeth's through a broken basement window that opened into an abandoned part of the hospital. We trudged through two inches of water, passed a statue of a Virgin Mary, and found the old children's ward. Abandoned board games with pieces missing; and photographs of doctors who practiced there in the early '30s; and on hangers in dusty closets, nurses' uniforms. Everything left the way it had been the last time someone walked these hallways.

Long-term effects of nuclear warfare.

A hallway exit sign no longer lit save the letter X, which remained a brilliant scarlet. The two of us pointing out things and making out every few feet.

Wrote my name in a layer of dust on a chalkboard.

The curtain in the confessional of the hospital's now-closed chapel is purple. The guy sat on the priest's side, and I sat on the supplicant's side, all bless me father and forgive me my sins and tell me how many Hail Marys will keep me out of hell. He asked me to take off my clothes, and I did.

We sat in a pew, waiting for the time to be right and the light to be right, and the guy lit a marijuana cigarette. Its smell took me back to Jay's bedroom, he at his computer desk watching weather—lightning, snow, green masses for rain—and me in his bed, wanting him to join me.

The guy asked me if I wanted some. I said no.

That initial weekend at St. Elizabeth's, I felt like I was shattering like light. I returned to the scene of the crime, where I started picking up and putting back together my demolished house of cards.

But with this man, I chased and caught shattered and reflected light. He took several pictures of a crucifix and a stained glass window. He asked me if I wanted to pose. I stood there, arms stretched wide, the way I stretch my arms wide when Avery asks how much I love him. Caught the light, dreamed a little dream, and then the light was gone, and the photographer asked if I wanted to have sex.

His mouth and fingers smelled like marijuana, and I think I told him yes less because it would be with him and more because of who I could pretend he was.

196

A woman made of diamonds, when she feels useless, has herself valued. I go on dates and have sex with strangers to feel valuable.

I saw him once more after our break-in, long enough to collect copies of the photographs of me. I'm mostly in shadow, but the light coming in through the stained glass created a stunning tableau.

2

Months later, just past the second anniversary of the day I met Jay, I Google Jay's name. I just want to peek and see what I can see. He locked his Twitter account, no longer uses his MySpace account, deleted his Facebook account, and stopped reviewing movies for an online site.

But there he is as surviving his mother. A couple of obituaries, one that appeared in a newspaper and the other linked to an online memorial guestbook. One person signed it, her ex-husband, Jay's father. This woman who I didn't know, but was slated to one day meet, has been dead for more than a year.

The fifth search result Google returns is an obituary posted by a funeral home in Olathe, Kansas for someone with Jay's name who is Jay's age who is survived by Jay's sister.

He died at home eight days before Aurora's first birthday.

He left behind loving friends.

His body was cremated.

Details about funeral arrangements are forthcoming.

No matter my combination of search terms, I can't find additional details about his death. No memorial guestbook to sign. No request for donations in lieu of flowers.

3

"If I found out I had one month to live, I'd rent the most expensive flat here and max out as many credit cards as I could get," Jay said the night he and I took Avery for ice cream, back when I thought he and I would work things out. His mother was starting chemotherapy. He was thinking about buying a car. He bought our ice cream, even though I offered to pay. The flats on this stretch of Newbury Street—on the entirety of Newbury and the surrounding streets—are expensive. "I'd want to live here, just to see what living like this feels like."

He said flat, not apartment, so I use flat, not apartment.

"No you wouldn't," I said. "You'd travel. There are all those places you've never been. Why would you stay still, if you knew you were dying? Why wouldn't you cram as much living as you could into however long you had left?"

"You know me too well," he said. "Of course I'd want to see the world."

"I'd go with you," I said, "if you knew you only had one month to live."

"I'll hold you to that," he said.

"What would you do?" he asked.

"I'd spend every day with Avery and Aurora."

Don't Walk became Walk, and the three of us crossed a street.

"You'd be back," Jay said. "We all come back."

I'd forget Jay's Buddhist beliefs and how he didn't believe in God until he said something like *we all come back.*

"What would you come back as?" I asked. A red light. Traffic crossing in front of us. Avery drinking out of his sippy cup. The sun already having set.

"I'd want to come back as someone who knows you."

4

Every year, about 700 million people travel by air. Suppose that half check a bag, or each year, 350 million pieces of luggage are checked. On average, one percent of all checked luggage goes unclaimed, so about 3.5 million bags end up taken to an unclaimed baggage center in Scottsboro, Alabama. There, everything is for sale. Cameras. Computers. Purses. Strollers. Crutches. Wheelchairs. Jewelry. Wedding dresses.

The warehouse where these things live is as cavernous as the warehouse at the end of *Raiders of the Lost Ark*; it is also a state tourist attraction. Its owners have operated this warehouse of forgotten or lost luggage for more than 40 years. More than 800,000 people come each year looking for deals. They can be found, if you're lucky.

That box in my closet—Emotional Baggage: Do Not Open—seems insignificant in comparison. I unbury it from the boxes stacked in front of it. I put inside the key to Jay's childhood bedroom home and notes and cards he gave me, his familiar handwriting telling me how much he loves me and how long we'll be together. I add the CDs he made and copies of photographs he took, phone numbers for his friends that I used when organizing his party, and a ticket stub to a movie we saw on our seventh or eighth date.

How much would someone pay in Scottsboro if I packed that box in a bag, checked it during a flight, and left it circling on the luggage carousel? Not that much, likely.

The box unpacked, its items no longer baggage, just things I claimed along the way.

5

He's not dead. He knows someone at this funeral home, and got him or her to post this untrue obituary. It's meant for me. He wants me to think he's dead. If I think he's dead, then I'll never try to get in touch with him. He's not dead. Someone would have let me know. He loved me. We were engaged. If he had died, I would have known.

I text Holly about another accidentally uncovered obituary, and she calls.

"How did you find out?" she asks.

"The obituary is online," I say.

"Where?" she asks, and I text her the link.

She reads it, while on the phone with me, and she cries.

"I'm so sorry," she says.

"I'm also not sure that he's dead," I say. "I can't find anything else about his death online."

I'm not the only ex-boyfriend he'd want to avoid, I think. He could have planted the obituary because of someone he dated after me.

I held his past, up until the point our future possibility ended; no matter the stories about his life after me that I made up, I'd never know if he easily moved on and if he

200

easily replaced me and if he ever found a different job. I'd know nothing except for the things I continue to carry.

"You think he'd do that?"

"I wouldn't be surprised."

"I'm just kind of in shock," Holly says. "I feel so sorry for him."

"I know," I say. "Me too."

"Are you OK?" Holly asks again.

"I'm fine," I say.

"You know this isn't your fault," Holly says.

"I know," I say, though I think I am partly to blame.

The decisions he and I separately made to end up in the same place at the same time, without knowing he and I were on a collision course.

I can hear Aurora start to cry. Holly will need to tend to our daughter.

"Call me if you need me," she says.

"I will," I say. "Thank you for calling me."

Holly texts later. She has been Googling for information about Jay, and came up with an article about a student in Florida with Jay's name who made honor roll in the third grade. At the time the article was written, he would have been in the third grade. But in the stories he told me about his life, he'd never mentioned a stint going to school in Florida. Which he would have told me, since I grew up in Florida.

"I don't think that's him," I say. "He didn't live in Florida."

"But who else has his name?" Holly says. "What if he made up his entire life? What if he wasn't who he told you he was?"

"I don't think so," I say. "He would have had to keep so many details straight."

"You were able to," Holly says. "What if he was doing the same thing?"

"I don't think so," I repeat.

But he could have invented a past, and invented a boarding school in England, and invented his British accent. I suppose his reinvention isn't outside the realm of possibility, given the lengths he took at the end of our relationship.

"It's him. I know that that was him in Florida," she says. "I get, now, how crazy he made you feel, and why you thought you had no other choice but to record him, if only to show him who you thought he was, because this is all crazy talk. That he would have made up his past, and made up his death. And that his doing that is possible."

6

In the morning, I call the Olathe police department. The woman who transfers me says the actual detective who worked the case can talk to me.

"How can I help you?" the detective asks, after introducing himself.

"I'm trying to find out information about someone who died last month," I say. I give him Jay's name and the date of death, and I wait for the detective to tell me that no one with that name has died.

But the detective doesn't need to look up the details about Jay's death.

"Yes," the detective says. "The coroner ruled his death a suicide."

Maybe Jay has a friend who works at the police station who could have faked the report. Maybe Jay told the

202

police to say he was dead, if anyone called looking for information about him.

"How did he die?" I ask. "Was it an accident?"

"I can't tell you that information," the detective says.

"I'm going to get in touch with his family, and I'd like to know the more appropriate thing to say: I'm sorry for your loss, or, I hope he's finally at peace."

"I can't tell you anything more than that the coroner ruled his death a suicide," the detective says.

I can't think of how I can get the detective to tell me more information.

I call the funeral home that handled the cremation, but they know less than the detective. Then I call the editor of a newspaper in Olathe and ask if there is anything in the paper about a suicide that occurred on the day Jay died. The editor digs through the archives and calls back. The paper never ran an obituary or death notice for anyone with Jay's name. There's no way of knowing more than what I know now. I'll have to fill in the blanks, a new type of mad lib, filled with adverbs and adjectives and dirty words best whispered.

That's it then. No one else to call.

7

I go to the park near where he worked. The wish-you-wonder bench has been stained a different color. I light a sandalwood candle. Jay burned this candle's twin on the night we met. He gave me this votive during our second date, when I asked him about the candle that he had burned during our first date.

I told him I would save that candle and burn it when he least expected it.

Its scent is a time machine, and I am back in Jay's room.

He's searching my pockets for chocolate and mocking my choice of wine and inviting me to dig through his music library. He's sitting in his bed waiting for me to make a move, and I'm sitting at the chair at his computer desk waiting for him to do the same.

The candle burns. Occasionally, the flame flickers. I hear the sound of a train passing nearby. Overhead lights in the parking lot turn on. Someone honks a horn.

A lover's game we used to play.

If you could choose the way you die, what would you choose?

Not by water and not by fire.

I said the same thing each time he'd ask.

Why not?

You'd know what was happening, and you wouldn't be able to stop it.

But it would be over and then it would be done.

I think I'd want something slow and drawn out.

I'd stop here. So would he. We'd talk about something else.

But I've thought a lot about it, especially since—

Well, since.

Do you want your end to be heart-attack quick or cancer slow?

Not sure which is better—having no time to say goodbye or feeling like all you do every day is say goodbye.

How would you want to die? I should know the answer to this by now.

He and I were double helixes of night and fire. We were the cancer and the heart attack. Each I love you—a goodbye in disguise.

Someone calls and then someone else texts. I turn off my cell phone. And then I turn on my cell phone.

I select the photo album on my phone filled with photos of Jay and Avery, and I press the delete button.

Are you sure?

I tell myself that I'll go after the candle burns itself out.

Acknowledgments

These acknowledgments will be true but inadequate. Words cannot express my gratitude, not just for how much people believed in the project but for how little they judged it.

Some of the material herein appeared previously, in different form, in other publications. I am grateful to the editors at the following publications for believing in *Second Person, Possessive*: *50 to 1*, *Absinthe Revival*, *Annalemma Magazine*, *The Brave New World*, *Bluestem Magazine*, *Cactus Heart*, *Cobalt Review*, *Curbside Quotidian*, *Daring to Repair*, *Dark Sky Magazine*, *Dr. Hurley's Snake-Oil Cure*, *Eunoria Review*, *The Fix*, *The Good Men Project*, *Ham Literature*, *Heavy Feather Review*, *Hippocampus Magazine*, *Inertia Magazine*, *Mixitini Matrix*, *Nontrue*, *Orange Quarterly*, *The Other Man*, *Peripheral Surveys+*, *Prick of the Spindle*, *Red Fez*, *Revolution House*, *The Rumpus*, *Sea Giraffe Magazine*, *Shaking Magazine*, *Smoking Poet*, *Specter Literary Magazine*, *Subterranean Literary Journal*, *This Great Society*, *Uptown Mosaic Magazine*, *Used Furniture Review*, *The Whistling Fire*, *Write This*, *The Writing Disorder*, *Xenith*, and *Zouch Magazine*.

I am also grateful to Gregory, Christy, Ken, Leslie, Tammy, James, and Eryn for reading early drafts.

Thank you to Shaun for the chicken wings, Niagara Falls, and for agreeing to one day go to Pumpkinland.

Second Person, Possessive would not be what it is today without the help of my friend, Mallory. She listened to my ramblings, reminded me that love, regardless of gender, is universal, and read and re-read the book so many times that she can quote whole sections. She holds keys to locks that I don't even know about and can tell you where all of the skeletons are buried.

Thank you also to my mother for the Shel Silverstein books when I was 12 and for always encouraging me.

Thank you to Avery and Aurora for occupying themselves while I worked, giving me much-needed time to disappear down rabbit holes of my own making. And a second thank you for Avery, especially, who saved me when I needed saving, often by simply putting his hand on my heart and asking what was wrong.

And a thank you to Holly for agreeing to let me tell this story. For that and for so much else, I am grateful.

About the author

William Henderson is a Pushcart Prize-nominated, Boston-based writer. He has written for the Advocate, is the former editor of The New England Blade, and is included in the 2012 Best Gay Writing anthology. His work has appeared in *Thought Catalog*, *The Huffington Post*, *The Good Men Project*, *Life By Me*, and other journals and magazines. His work has been translated into three languages.

Second Person, Possessive is his first book.

www.ingramcontent.com/pod-product-compliance
Lightning Source LLC
LaVergne TN
LVHW011226080426
835509LV00005B/346